Plant
Tribe

Editor: Shawna Mullen
Designer: Heesang Lee
Production Manager: Denise LaCongo

Library of Congress Control Number: 2019939902

ISBN: 978-1-4197-4041-1
eISBN: 978-1-68335-876-3

Text copyright © 2020 Igor Josifovic and Judith de Graaff
Photographs copyright © 2020 Jules Villbrandt

Cover © 2020 Abrams

Published in 2020 by Abrams, an imprint of ABRAMS.
All rights reserved. No portion of this book may be reproduced,
stored in a retrieval system, or transmitted in any form or by
any means, mechanical, electronic, photocopying, recording,
or otherwise, without written permission from the publisher.

Printed and bound in China
10 9 8 7 6 5 4

Abrams books are available at special discounts when purchased
in quantity for premiums and promotions as well as fundraising
or educational use. Special editions can also be created to
specification. For details, contact specialsales@abramsbooks.com
or the address below.

Abrams® is a registered trademark of Harry N. Abrams, Inc.

ABRAMS The Art of Books
195 Broadway, New York, NY 10007
abramsbooks.com

Plant Tribe

living happily ever after with plants

Igor Josifovic & Judith de Graaff

photography by Jules Villbrandt

Abrams, New York

Love is the essence of life. It drives us, challenges us, makes life beautiful—and sometimes transforms it into a roller-coaster ride, complete with ups and downs and crazy loops. Through it all, love is what keeps us going and shapes us. Love also demands that we nurture it: It is based on giving and receiving. And all this rings true for our love for plants as well as people.

As you flip through this book, read the chapters, and look at the photos, keep in mind: Love is the spirit of this book. *Plant Tribe* is a book filled with love, good vibes, happiness, and creativity. It invites you on a journey of discovery and experimentation, soul-searching and nurturing, and into a shared and deep affection for plants.

Books and articles about how to keep your houseplants healthy and thriving abound, but we aimed to bring a little more to our readers: We wanted to offer perspective—and to celebrate how much plants bring to the lives of all who welcome them into their homes. With that mission in mind, we traveled the world—visiting inspiring people, talking to them about their bond with plants, and hearing stories that made us laugh out loud and moved us to tears.

We discovered that plants play a key role in well-being, positive energy, happiness, love, and creativity. Join us, and travel through each chapter of this book, in the company of the Plant Tribe, a global movement of plant lovers. Since this book has found its way into your hands, you are now part of the tribe, too. Our shared love of plants unites us from every corner of the world.

Plants teach us one important lesson: Life changes with the seasons. Every moment has a reason, and every low will eventually pass. Embrace your love of plants as you embrace life, which is all around us, buzzing, blooming, and thriving. Welcome to the Plant Tribe, friend!

Igor Josifovic & Judith de Graaff
@urbanjungleblog——urbanjunglebloggers.com

chapter 1

LOVE
YOUR
PLANTS

The faces of a happy, global Plant Tribe.

There is one key element for happy and thriving plants, superseding even light, water, or soil. It is love. Everything starts and ends with love. It is the alpha and omega of any relationship—the relationship with your partner, your family, yourself, or your plants. Love is the principle that will guide you in your life with plants.

It's in our human nature to nourish the world around us with love. Whatever is devoid of love will wither, wilt, and, eventually, die. But to be able to give love, we need to love and care for ourselves. Understanding the importance of love and self-care is essential, no matter what our actions or intentions.

It's easy to get off track: We love this home, we love this trip, we love this shirt—social media can make the list of things we desire almost endless. It can even make the lives of others seem much better than our own. Yes, on Instagram even the plants of another person can seem so much nicer, so much healthier than our own! But what we see is a distorted image, presented to us in perfect bite-size portions on our ever-buzzing smartphones.

So this chapter is here as a gentle reminder: To love fully and sincerely, you must first love yourself. Once you succeed, you can share the nourishing power of love with other living things—including your plants.

love, self-care, and plants

Plants need light, water, soil—but they also need our presence.

Your level of love and self-care is as crucial to your relationship with houseplants as it is to the other parts of your life. It will enhance your emotional bond with your plants and mark the beginning of a long and thriving green relationship.

Take a few minutes to work through the following four points in order to heighten your understanding of self-care, love, and emotional bonding with your plants.

AWARENESS

Become aware of yourself and your entire being. Take note of your senses, your body, and your mind. Close your eyes and take a moment to be aware of who you are and where you are. Feel your surroundings with your fingertips. Once you feel centered and present, focus on your plants. Which was the last plant you acquired? Why did you choose it? Which plant is currently not happy? Are you aware of your plants and your plants' needs? Sometimes we forget our plants and they become mere decorative elements in our homes. But they are more than decor. They are living beings and deserve our full awareness—at least when we're at home, surrounded by them.

Try this:

- Count, in your head, the number of plants you have at home (you can count in dozens, if that helps).
- Recall the last plant you parted with.
- Remember the last surprise you received from one of your plants.

APPRECIATION

Humans and plants have the same roots. We all come from nature. This natural bond ties us together as a family (in a way that can never be achieved with objects) and deserves our full appreciation. You may wish to direct your appreciation toward nature as a whole or to plants in their natural habitats and in your own home—the urban jungle you created.

Try this:

- Think of a plant that made you smile recently and be thankful.
- Remember the last time you walked in nature and had a feeling of gratitude.
- Appreciate your plants for being your kin—fellow children of nature.

PRESENCE

Plants thrive on the energy we transmit not only when we care for them but whenever we are in their company. Plants are nourished by our presence as much as they are by water and nutrients from the soil. Abandoned plants will wither or grow gnarly and unhappy. Left alone in a pot in a cold hallway, would you be thriving happily? No—nor will a plant. Rotating plants from little-used areas and carving out some time for our green roommates will help fuel them with the positive energy that imbues a space with life.

Try this:

- Put aside time for your plants and spend it consciously in their presence (read, draw, sip a cup of coffee, meditate, do yoga, whatever you like).
- Make it a daily ritual—your sacred me-time in the presence of your plants.
- Move plants from rarely frequented corners of your home to lived-in spaces.

CONTENTMENT

Be content in the company of your plants. Remind yourself to pay attention to the positive effect plants have on your mood. Disconnect from the daily hassle and focus on your green friends for a short moment every day. Sit down, sip a cup of coffee, and feel the contentment of a life among happy and thriving green company.

Reminding yourself about the magic of love will help you set the tone for a long-lasting and happy green home. As living creatures, plants will return your love and show their appreciation in healthy growth, thriving leaves, or lush flowers.

bonding with your plants

Take your time and pay attention to your plants' sign language, and respond appropriately.

Creating a close bond with your plants will help both you and them thrive. Here's a simple trick: Instead of using them as decorative objects, start thinking of your plants as green roommates. And these roommates deserve our friendship—after all, we share a home together! These bonds are easy to create, from simply naming your plants to initiating daily rituals with them.

Fred the fiddle fig and
Susie the snake plant.
Just an idea! But why
not? Name your plants!

NAMING YOUR PLANTS

We've heard many names for beloved plants, including Andrea the Giant (a *Euphorbia trigona*), Marvin (a *Ficus elastica*), and Fish (a *Dracaena*). Giving names to your plants or to one outstanding, special plant creates an immediate bond. The plant becomes almost like a member of your family, and your awareness of its needs and happiness is heightened.

TALKING TO YOUR PLANTS

There are lots of theories concerning the positive effects of playing music to—or talking to—plants. In simple greenhouse experiments, where plants were exposed to positive or negative speech, classical or heavy metal music—or even complete silence—the results were evident, though perhaps not completely scientific. (In case you're wondering: Talking was the second most effective, while the heavy metal music produced the fastest plant growth, so go and check your home music collection!) Some researchers assume that the release of carbon dioxide (exhaled during speech) stimulates plant growth. Whatever the reason, let's just say that a good deal of positive talk (and, perhaps, some music) can't do your plants any harm! And if they thrive thanks to your encouraging words, what other proof do you need?

LISTENING TO YOUR PLANTS

It's one thing to name your plants and talk to them. But do not underestimate the power of listening, too. Obviously, plants will not talk to you the way we human beings talk to one another, but they will send out signals. Maybe your plant is bending over toward the light? Move it to a brighter spot! Maybe your plant is curling its leaves? Water it again! Perhaps your plant has lost its shine and looks a bit under the weather? Take it to the bathroom and give it a refreshing and cleansing shower!

love your plants

living with
plants and pets

If you are lucky, your pets are not interested in plants at all, like Lemon.

What makes a house a home are the living beings you surround yourself with—your partner (who could not care less about your plants but secretly enjoys the calming effect of all the greenery at home), your kids (who help you take care of your houseplants), or your roommates or best friends (who steal a little cutting when they come over for pizza). But what about your furry friends? Cats and dogs are an important part of many families and contribute to the dynamics of a home. They have their own favorite places to sleep and play. They like to be fed on time, or even all the time. And sometimes they like to feed themselves and take bites out of your plants! Help! That's where things become interesting: Living successfully with plants and pets can be very challenging, but there's no reason the two can't coexist. It requires patience, tact, compromise on occasion, and some handy tips and tricks to keep everyone at home safe, happy, and healthy.

First of all, you know your pet best. If your furry friend doesn't care about plants and leaves them alone, then lucky you! Many cats and dogs have an appetite for new, exciting things, however, and enjoy playing with items like feathers, flowers, soil, leaves, or entire plants. Some houseplants are even extra attractive for pets: The leaves of spider plants, banana plants, and palms are particularly delicious because of their sweet, juicy taste. And while these are not dangerous for your pets (except for sago palms and cycads), a plant with a little bite out of it doesn't look very good. And before you know it, there may not be any leaves left.

TEACH THEM

Like humans, pets can be taught how to behave (although the success rate is not the same for every cat or dog). On average, the younger the pet, the easier it is to regulate his behavior. While it may not be simple, you can try to teach your pet not to play with your plants. First, observe your pet's behavior around the plants: Is he looking for a spot to chill, is he just being playful, or is he trying to get your attention by tapping on some leaves?

It is important to be consistent and let pets know it's not OK when they harm plants. Depending on your pet parenting style, you can use a squirt from a spray bottle filled with water to warn them away from your plants, but in most cases this isn't necessary: Simply talking to them and repeating that they shouldn't misbehave is usually enough. Unfortunately, not all of us can be with our pets the whole day, so correcting bad behavior consistently is not always an option. This is where our handy tips and tricks can help you avoid a plant disaster.

PLANTS CAN KILL

Houseplants should not be considered pet food, even if your cat or dog has a different opinion: Some taste very good or help their digestive systems. Many of the most common houseplants are, instead, poisonous when ingested by our pets. They can cause vomiting and gastrointestinal upset. Never assume that pets instinctively know which plants are toxic to them. Our cats and dogs are domesticated animals, and knowing what is good or bad for them is not necessarily part of their experience. Some pets are not interested in plants at all and can be left alone in a room with toxic plants without any problem, but if you're the parent of a cat or dog who loves to nibble on fresh plant leaves, make sure to avoid the toxic plants listed on page 19.

Like humans, pets can be taught to behave around plants. Goldendoodle Lemon is a perfect example.

17

left: Cats are sometimes attracted by all the foliage, but some cats, like Kittie here, will listen when their owner tells them not to touch the plants.

below: With a little patience, even active pets—like Jack Russell Mylee—can be taught to live in harmony with plants.

PLANTS TOXIC TO PETS

- *Aloe*
- *Anthurium*
- Any bulbous plants, such as lilies, hyacinths, daffodils, and amaryllis
- Asparagus ferns
- *Azalea*
- *Dieffenbachia*
- *Dracaena*
- *Monstera deliciosa*
- *Oxalis triangularis*
- Sago palms and other cycads
- *Sansevieria*
- *Zamioculcas*

This list is not complete, so always check to see if your plants are toxic.
    The ASPCA keeps an updated list on its website: http://urbnjn.gl/Toxic-Untoxic-Plants. While, with most plants, your pet would have to ingest a substantial amount to become ill, any plant material may cause your pet to vomit or have gastrointestinal issues. Better to be safe than sorry.

PLANTS SAFE FOR PETS

- Cacti (though their spines can hurt!)
- *Calathea*
- *Echeveria* and *Haworthia* succulents
- Ferns
- Grasses
- Kentia palms (some cats love to eat juicy, sweet palm leaves, which destroys the plants)
- Lemon and olive trees
- Lemongrass
- *Maranta*
- *Peperomia* (cats don't like the taste!)
- Spider plants
- Staghorn ferns
- *Tillandsia* air plants

This poodle prefers chilling to playing with plants.

AVOID PLANT DOMINOES

Make sure your flowerpots cannot fall over and create chain-reaction catastrophes. Here's a made-up example: Your dog is excited when you come home from work and is a bit unruly. You've placed your cactus plant on a bench in the hallway, and one day, when your dog comes to greet you, the cactus gets tipped over, the spines stick you and your pet, the pot breaks into pieces, and the cactus is all banged up—a domino disaster! Or maybe you have a cat who loves to jump on every high shelf in the house and walk in between all your belongings. You can avoid damage to the plant (or even that precious trinket) you placed up there by securing it on the shelf: Simply move the plant against the wall so that your kitty can skirt it, or make a hole in the shelf that is slightly smaller in diameter than the widest part of the flowerpot. The hole will hold your pot in place and adds an unexpected twist to your shelf.

Falls will also occur when top-heavy plants sit in pots that are too light or too small. Heavier plants, especially large succulents and cacti, need heavy ceramic or terra-cotta pots to keep them steady, so pay attention to the containers as your plants grow. If you aren't ready to repot, you can set a plant close to the wall and secure it by wrapping some nice ribbons around the pot and anchoring them to the wall. In general, it's a good idea to allow enough space around plants for the circulation of air and the movement of people and pets. When your dog wags his tail, you don't want him to tip over a plant on your coffee table.

opposite: Avoid damage to plants by securing them on a shelf or by making sure the plant pots are sturdy and not easy to tip over.

right: A happy and tired animal will leave your plants alone.

KEEP THEM ACTIVE!

Give your pets an activity center—a nice scratching post and catnip-filled play mice for cats, a nice bone or squeaky toy for your dog. And play with your pets to tire them out. In general, cats are a little bit naughtier than dogs. Give your feline friends their own cat grass, catnip, edible foliage, or wheat grass. Place this close to your nontoxic plants at ground level, so that they have easy access, before they reach your precious houseplants. If your cat has a favorite (nontoxic) houseplant, buy him one of his own that he is free to destroy. And place your perfect plant out of reach. Make sure to prune plants regularly so that they don't get leggy and become tempting toys for your pets. In addition, some animals love to play in or drink the water from plant saucers. Avoid a water ballet by emptying plant trays after you water. Finally, keep bottles, vases, and glassware in which you're propagating cuttings out of reach. Pets may fish the baby plants out of the water so that they can drink (because, yes, they may find this water tastier than the water in their own bowls).

above, left: Like many pets, Baunilha loves human attention but she doesn't care about the plants.

above, right: Alina (see page 194) taught Sofie not to nibble her plants—and a lot of other tricks, too, like "roll over," "high five," and "kiss"!

right: Despite living among a large collection of tropical plants, some of which are toxic to cats, Sofie knows not to chew on the leaves or destroy them.

SECURE YOUR PLANTS

If you have acrobatic pets or cannot keep them from destroying your plants, there are a few solutions, including keeping plants out of their reach—whether on a high shelf, on top of the fridge, hanging from the ceiling, or in a planter mounted on the wall. Your toxic plants can be kept in a room that is off-limits to pets, like a bathroom or bedroom. Fragile plants can be kept in a terrarium or tabletop greenhouse. Another tip is to find a scent that your pet intensely dislikes, like citrus. Leave some slices of citrus fruit around the area where you keep your plants, or on the soil of each individual pot. This should deter your pet from wanting to play with, eat, or otherwise destroy your plants.

What to do when your pet loves to dig in the soil of your flowerpots, or even uses it as a litter box? Cut some chicken wire and lay it flat on top of the soil, to cover it. This will prevent your furry friend from digging up the soil or roots and making a huge mess. You can also use some large stones or gemstones to partly cover the soil. Just keep in mind that pets can find small stones or shells equally interesting to play with.

AND A FINAL NOTE

Accept that your pet will nibble on some of your houseplants and that they may show some scars. Learn to live with your imperfect plants. After all, it's your pet's home, too!

love your plants

If you have an acrobatic pet, keep plants well above where your pet can jump or climb (as Andy does for his Ragdoll cat, Cavanaugh).

plant tribe stories . . .
Julie Hagan

"You've never known a plant until
you've killed it three times."

Location

Little Compton, Rhode Island, USA

Profession

Billing consultant

Zodiac

Sagittarius

Lives with

Husband Brooks, sons Asa and William,
cats Pippi and Shadow

House size

2,800 square feet / 260 square meters

Favorite plant

Begonias

Plant decor idea

More is better! Group lots of plants
together—it looks better and it is better
for the plants, too.

Number of plants

More than 600

Instagram

@farm.coast.house.plants

left: The sunroom features Julie's vast collection of plants, including a true plant throne.

below, left: The sunroom is also called the Florida room, for obvious reasons: It's a space for thriving beauties, like these *Begonia* and *Pilea* plants.

bottom, left: The charming Rhode Island dwelling of Julie's family.

bottom, right: Begonias make up the majority of Julie's collection, but there are also quite a few spiky specimens on display.

On the shores of the Atlantic Ocean, in a small village in the tiny state of Rhode Island, a charming and spacious farmhouse is home to Julie's planty family. The previous owner of the property was also passionate about gardening, so the grounds are landscaped with a double pond and stone walls of varying heights (to bridge the uneven plot). Inside the house, a large sunroom was designed as a dedicated room for plants (like an indoor greenhouse.) The minute she saw it, Julie knew that this was the perfect place to raise her family (as well as her ever-growing collection of begonias).

She first discovered her passion for plants while working at a restaurant and trying her hand at growing and cooking her own produce. After that, she experimented with growing unusual fare and supplying it to chefs. She got even more hooked on plants when her husband gifted her with a begonia. Slowly, she began collecting more and more. "I really got into it and today I am a member of the American Begonia Society and the Boston Begonia Society."

Although she has well over six hundred plants, Julie spends just three hours a week caring for her collection. "The plants are grouped together so it is fairly easy to care for them. The fussier ones are wick watered [this is done by burying one end of a fabric string or cord in the plant's soil and hanging the other end in a vessel of water; the water will travel through the string and be absorbed by the plant], which is simple and also doesn't take much time."

While the majority of plants in the sunroom are begonias, there are also quite a few spiky specimens on display because her son William is a cactus fan. He collects cacti and succulents and he even got Julie interested in some (although she is not as big a fan as he is). "He got me into jungle cacti, epiphytic cacti, and I really like them. His favorite cactus is Old-Man cactus a *Cephalocereus senilis*."

Another special plant in the collection is a Norfolk Island pine (*Araucaria heterophylla*). "Brooks got it from his grandmother, and we nursed it slowly back to health." This inspired Julie to launch an Instagram series called Heirloom Plants: plants that cross decades and are passed on to a new generation, helping keep the memories of loved ones alive. It makes them extra special. However, inheritance is not the only way to add new plants to your collection without spending a lot. "I joined two plant societies that allowed me to learn a lot of new things about begonias from fellow members. It is also where I can get ahold of plants for a nominal amount."

A peek at Julie's collection of succulents and cacti, including a tall *Bryophyllum daigremontianum*.

Theodora Melnik

"If there were no plants in my home,
it would not be home."

Location

Berlin, Germany

Profession

Copywriter

Zodiac

Taurus

Lives with

Boyfriend Benjamin and cats Miro and
Charlie

Apartment size

688 square feet / 64 square meters

Favorite plant

Monstera deliciosa

Plant decor idea

Group lots of plants together in a
variety of different sizes, shapes, and
colors.

Number of plants

Approximately 130

Instagram

@_____theo

Berlin's Neukölln district is rough around the edges but home to many hip bars and cool coffee places. It's also where creative couple Theodora and Benjamin live. Their cozy apartment is located in an old building with lots of charming details. Stepping through the door feels like a voyage through time: The apartment seems to encapsulate the true spirit of old Berlin. Vintage details wherever you look, a bike in the living room, thrifted furniture, plaster walls—plus more than one hundred houseplants filling the space with good energy.

While the cats, Miro and Charlie, seem unimpressed by guests, Theo and Benjamin prove to be excellent hosts. A homemade vanilla cake with cape gooseberries is on the table, fresh coffee is brewing in the kitchen, and we are welcomed with a smile. The love and positive energy are palpable.

"Thanks to our plants, we truly live a harmonious life," says Theo. "I think all the nature in our home creates that extra dose of positive energy—for us and for our cats," she adds. A blended family of pets and plants is not an issue at all in this charming space; plants that cats find tempting (like *Dracaena*) are simply avoided, so everyone can coexist happily.

True to the spirit of their home, Theo and Benjamin revel in new growth. "Every new leaf makes me so happy—it really fuels my body . . . That's why I high-five my plants when they grow a new leaf. And sharing my happiness with Benjamin creates such a positive atmosphere. Our thriving plants are a beautiful example of our bond as a couple," says Theo. We can only agree. Here's to love and happiness!

opposite, top left: A homemade vanilla cake decorated with cape gooseberries.

opposite, top right: Plant shelfie with a *Hoya carnosa,* asparagus fern, *Rhipsalis baccifera, Sansevieria, Rhipsalis ramulosa,* and a small *Sparrmannia africana.*

opposite, bottom: An avocado seed never goes to waste in Theo and Benjamin's home: They always grow them into a new plant in the windowsill.

above: The midcentury sideboard holds part of Theo's large collection of plants.

Toy Taniel

"There is always room for more plants!"

Location

São Paulo, Brazil

Profession

Barista

Zodiac

Capricorn

Lives with

Solo

Apartment size

452 square feet / 42 square meters

Favorite plant

Philodendron spiritus-sancti and anthuriums in general

Plant decor idea

Spice up your shelves with many scattered plants!

Number of plants

Approximately 250

Instagram

@toy.taniel

Toy is a remarkable guy—he describes himself as a collector of unfinished tattoos and rare aroids. His small apartment is the epitome of an urban jungle—clean, white lines, sophisticated details, and tall skyscrapers all around—and in the middle there is Toy's lush green oasis with aroids that boast leaves the size of an adult human (look at the *Anthurium veitchii*).

Visits with Toy always include two of his passions: excellently brewed coffee and discussing plants. Toy is truly a plant hunter. His focus is on rare jungle species, aroids, that he chases throughout Brazil. Some of his plants are so unusual even botanical gardens would be envious.

His enormous love for plants also has a humorous side. "If I invite a date here and they are scared by the number of plants in my apartment—then the date is over," he says with a mischievous smile. We wonder: Who wouldn't want to date a plant guy who makes excellent coffee?

opposite: Toy posing with his huge *Anthurium veitchii*.

above: Toy's balcony is filled with an array of rare philodendrons and anthuriums.

left: Blending indoors and outdoors with a lush urban jungle is Toy's interior design guideline.

plant tribe stories . . .
Jennifer Wallace

"If you can spend less than an hour
when you visit a plant shop,
you are doing something wrong."

Location

Alexandria, Virginia, USA

Profession

Visual content creator and shop manager
at Little Leaf plant shop

Zodiac

Cancer

Lives with

Her sister and cats Snookie and Kittie

Apartment size

1,180 square feet / 110 square meters

Favorite plant

String of pearls

Plant decor idea

Make a terrarium lamp from a simple glass
jar and a lampshade (see page 180).

Number of plants

Approximately 200

Instagram

@jungleinaroom

Jennifer got interested in plants while decorating her first apartment. She discovered the Urban Jungle Bloggers through Pinterest and was instantly hooked: A photo of a bird-of-paradise in a living room caught her eye and she simply had to have that plant. "Despite knowing better (I work in a plant shop after all!), I put my first bird-of-paradise in a dark corner. It suffered hard and now I'm helping it recover!"

Throughout Jennifer's apartment, you notice plants everywhere. The bedroom is a sanctuary for *Calathea*, peace lilies, ZZ plants, *Alocasia*, and *Sansevieria*. The adjoining sunroom is another sweet spot, with dozens of plants thriving in the bright, mostly indirect sunlight. It all looks effortless and easygoing, which it totally is. "I water sporadically, although I check on my plants every evening when I get home. They remedy the hectic part of my day and always change my mood for the better. I am emotionally attached to them."

Jennifer's motto is to have fun with plants and "Don't get stressed out!" That motto is sometimes needed since she has two furry housemates, Snookie and Kittie, who are attracted to the foliage. "A little plant damage is hard to avoid when you live with cats, but overall we're doing well. They listen when I tell them not to touch, and they rarely tip over a pot."

opposite: Jennifer in her sunroom.

above: In a corner that was too dark for growing things, Jennifer made crates into plant displays by equipping them with flat-panel grow lights (see page 84).

left: Having plants in the bedroom doesn't only look good; it helps improve your quality of sleep as well.

chapter 2

GOOD ENERGY WITH PLANTS

How can we, as urban dwellers in the twenty-first century, bring the magic and energy of plant power into our homes?

To begin with, we have to be aware of one fact: We are made of energy. This energy is both physical and spiritual and nourishes our entire life. It influences our level of well-being, which is both physical and emotional. Energy is also flowing and in constant flux—it enters our homes and it leaves our homes. We should always aim to bring in more positive energy, however, and to get rid of negative vibes. One simple way to bring positive energy into our homes is plants.

Throughout human history, plants were thought to be magical sources of energy. People worshipped plants, personified them, and attributed power to them. Plants were sacred beings in the same hierarchy as humans and animals. Back in 1973 Peter Tompkins and Christopher Bird wrote an entire book, titled *The Secret Life of Plants*, about the physical, emotional, and spiritual relationship between humans and plants. In it, they delve into what they call "plant mysteries" and shed light on the physics and metaphysics of plants.

Nowadays we have lost much of what was so natural and sacred to our ancestors. We often value reason over emotion; we consider our human existence superior to nature. But our world is multilayered and multifaceted. In her recent book *The Enchanted Life: Unlocking the Magic of the Everyday*, Sharon Blackie notes how alive we might feel if we focused our awareness on these many and varied facets—including the world of rocks, animals, plants, soil, and weather that is all around us.

right: Bring your full
sensory attention to
what you're doing by
smudging sage. Be sure
to buy high-quality and
ethically sourced sage.

below and opposite:
Plants, sage, candles,
and crystals work
together to create good
vibes in a home.

above: Sometimes the
good energy is in the
details—like exceptional
plants or handmade
ceramics.

opposite and right:
Houseplants help focus
our awareness on nature,
making us feel more
energized and alive.

purify your home with plants

Plants help purify the air in the entire home, not only bathrooms.

It is widely known (and scientifically confirmed) that plants help purify the air in our homes. They not only absorb common household toxins from the air we breathe and release fresh oxygen but also positively impact the energy level in our homes by improving the overall living environment. Most plants have an air-purifying effect. Certain plants, however, are real power boosters for fresh air. They remove toxins that are emitted by synthetic materials and fibers in closed spaces (such as plastic, carpets, etc.), as well as by air pollution from outside. Here are six of our favorites:

DEVIL'S IVY OR GOLDEN POTHOS
(*EPIPREMNUM AUREUM*)

Not only is this one of the easiest houseplants to grow, it is also one of the superpower plants when it comes to clean air and positive vibes. Its cascading tendrils and its leaves of varying shapes and colors are an uplifting sight and fill your space with flowing energy. Pothos grows easily in pots, hanging baskets, and even in water.

Toxins removed:
benzene, formaldehyde,
trichloroethylene, and
xylene.

PHILODENDRON

Philodendron is a large genus of evergreen plants that are popular for growing indoors. Those with heart-shaped leaves, in particular, are a sheer delight: Their powerful green leaves ooze with positive energy. Most *Philodendron* species are fast growers and thrive in bright indirect light. They are ideal for growing as trailing plants—along shelves, door and window frames, and curtain rods—or simply climbing up your wall. The instant jungle effect elevates the mood and exerts both an invigorating and a calming power.

Toxin removed:
formaldehyde.

PEACE LILY
(*SPATHIPHYLLUM*)

This lush plant has all the positivity its name implies. It brings a sense of peace and harmony into your space with its oblong, deep green leaves and mostly white spathes (commonly mistaken for flowers). The actual flower grows as a spadix in the middle of the spathe. This beauty is another easy-to-care-for houseplant, and thrives in low-light conditions.

Toxins removed:
benzene, carbon monoxide,
formaldehyde, trichloroethylene, and xylene.

SNAKE PLANT
(SANSEVIERIA)

SPIDER PLANT
(CHLOROPHYTUM COMOSUM)

ALOE VERA

The snake plant has it all: It's harder to kill than to keep alive and it produces good vibes in any corner—even in the shade of a hallway. In the practice of feng shui, this plant, sometimes referred to as mother-in-law's tongue, is considered to have strong positive energies. It's a fantastic plant for bedrooms, as its consumption of carbon dioxide and release of oxygen during the night enhance the quality of sleep.

Toxins removed: benzene, formaldehyde, trichloroethylene, and xylene.

Some people consider spider plants common and unspectacular. This plant is a real source of joy, however. Owners of spider plants experience ongoing positive energy with this forgiving houseplant: It thrives with only minimal care and tends to produce many offshoots. The sight of its dangling babies will warm your heart and make you smile.

Toxins removed: formaldehyde and xylene.

This is not only a plant; it's a healer among plants. Aloe vera has been known throughout history for its healing properties and good energies. The gel from aloe vera leaves has anti-inflammatory properties for the body and soothing effects for the soul. To look at this plant and be aware of all the goodness it contains makes you appreciate nature even more. Aloes are not only strong air cleaners; they can also indicate the level of toxins in a room: Brown spots on their leaves could mean there are high amounts of harmful chemicals in the air.

Toxin removed: formaldehyde.

plants and crystals

This *Begonia rex* rocks good vibes, thanks to some rock crystals.

above: Scatter
crystals around
plant arrangements
for extra good
energy.

right: Negative
vibes don't stand
a chance thanks
to this chunky
amethyst.

Both plants and crystals are born from the one and only Mother Earth.

They are imbued with the powerful, ever-present energy of our planet. Gems and minerals originate deep within the earth's crust and, in their various shapes and colors, manifest the forces that created them. Crystals and all sorts of stones have been valued for their healing and magical powers for thousands of years. And even today, we have a strong connection to their power—sometimes consciously, other times unconsciously, for example, in our choice of special stones for jewelry. Crystals and gemstones fill our lives with magic—whether we wear them on our bodies or place them thoughtfully in our homes. But what about their connection to plants?

The earth nourishes plants; the earth makes crystals—it seems like a logical conclusion that plants and crystals have a strong bond and that crystals have a beneficial effect on our plants. How can we harness the good vibrations and energies of crystals for the growth and well-being of our plants?

First, we have to identify stones that are particularly beneficial. Here are a few suggestions to get you started with some crystal magic of your own:

CLEAR QUARTZ

This is the best and most versatile crystal to start with. It's considered one of the most spiritually healing crystals, with abundant powers. Clear quartz is connected to transformation, clarity, healing, balance, and focus. This crystal enables a constant flow of energy: It amplifies and regulates energy levels, it cleanses and fends off negative vibes—and this is as true for you, your home, and your pets as it is for your plants.

AMETHYST

This purple crystallized quartz is known for its cleansing and purifying powers. It's also a crystal of protection and healing. Amethysts hold a soothing energy that calms and eases the mind. With its wide energy field, an amethyst placed among plants will help cleanse the surrounding area of negative vibes.

ROSE QUARTZ

This pale pink stone is popular and an excellent crystal to use in the home. It is often referred to as the "stone of love" and is considered essential for nurturing and healing. It soothes the body and mind and helps open the heart to new experiences. Rose quartz is also believed to promote fertility and thus can help your plants thrive and grow. Support young plants, cuttings, and offshoots especially with a rose quartz.

SMOKY QUARTZ

Smoky quartz crystals come in various shades, from translucent to opaque brown, and have a strong connection to the earth. They are famous for their grounding powers and for energy transmutation. They divert negativity and leave a clean space for growth and stabilization. Smoky quartz is a great crystal to help strengthen ailing plants.

above: Gems and minerals
originate deep within the
earth's crust and, in their
various shapes and colors,
manifest the forces that
created them.

left: Clear quartz is one of
the most powerful crystals:
Place little quartz pieces
next to plants to boost
their energy levels.

opposite: Symbols of all
kinds can raise energy, too.
Here, a neon statue stands
guard over a *Begonia rex*.

CITRINE

This member of the quartz family comes in soft to bright yellow or orange hues. It is connected to mental clarity, optimism, and regeneration. The citrine also promotes abundance, and is considered helpful when you want to let your creative juices flow. For lush growth, place a citrine close to your plants, but don't combine it with clear quartz, as the two together are too powerful.

MOSS AGATE

This green crystal is the most powerful of all agates and is often referred to as the crystal of farmers and gardeners. It's said to bring abundance and prosperity, and to strengthen the connection to the earth. Use a moss agate or a group of them around your plants—they will benefit from the crystal's powerful energy and will respond with health and vitality.

AMAZONITE

Amazonite is feldspar, which means it's a crystalline mineral. It's said to help us find harmony with others and with our environment, and it encourages speaking the truth and finding our flow and inspiration. Amazonite is also known for its balancing powers. It interacts well with plants and will help yours stay balanced and grounded.

PETALITE

This feldspar has a reputation as a high-vibration stone. It emits a high level of positive vibes and keeps negativity at bay. This stone helps us connect with the spiritual realm and balances the energy level in its vicinity. It's also considered a protective stone and has been used as a talisman throughout history. Petalite is said to relieve stress levels, so place one among your plants to keep the good vibes balanced and the negative, stressful energy away.

TOURMALINE

Protection, security, and stress relief are associated with tourmaline. This crystal comes in various dark shades, and black tourmaline is one of the most popular stones when it comes to positive effects. It's literally a bodyguard stone, cleansing negative energy wherever you place it—whether on your body as a piece of jewelry, in your car, next to your computer, or among your houseplants. If you want a strong purifier and cleanser to keep positive vibes in your home, go for a black tourmaline!

A rock from the
Moroccan Sahara Desert,
a smoky quartz, and
rock quartz placed in a
handmade fig leaf bowl.

APATITE

Although it is most commonly deep blue or green, apatite comes in a multitude of colors. It's a calcium phosphate mineral and a main source of phosphorus for plants, which makes it a great stone to put in your flowerpot: The plant will be energized directly through the soil. You can also use this stone to infuse water to drink yourself or for watering your plants!

Now that you have this list of crystals that are good for your plants in hand, it's time to consider how to use these crystals in order to transfer their good energy to your houseplants. Try one, a few, or all of these ideas:

Place crystals next to your plants

Sometimes the simplest idea is a good idea! Placing crystals next to your plants is an efficient and decorative way of imbuing your plants with the positive vibes exuded by crystals. Arrange a cluster of clear quartz next to your plants, and add smoky quartz, amethyst, or moss agate—play with the combinations. Just avoid combinations that are too strong, like clear quartz with citrine. This way your plants will get all the positive energy and your plant arrangement will sparkle and shine.

Put crystals in your flowerpot

This is the most powerful way to channel crystals' positive forces to your plants. By placing crystals in your flowerpot, you will fuel the plant with good energy. Be sure to use only suitable crystals, however, as the chemical constituents of certain crystals (lead or arsenic, for example) can be harmful to plants when dissolved in water. All crystals from the quartz family—clear quartz, amethyst, rose quartz, smoky quartz, and citrine—are chemically "clean," however, and can go directly into your flowerpot. These are compounds of silicon and oxygen (SiO_2), with minimal traces of iron, aluminum, or titanium. Various unpolished stones are also ideal for placing on top of soil: a pink petalite, an amazonite, apatites, or tourmalines, for example.

Wear or carry crystals while tending to your plants

Don't forget that crystals have a powerful energy field that you can carry with you—for example, while caring for your plants. Why not put a powerful and energy-packed crystal in your pocket or around your neck or wrist (as a piece of jewelry) while you minister to your plants? The positive vibes will radiate and make both you and your plants look beautiful and well energized!

Water your plants with crystal-infused water

If you're already a firm believer in the positive effects of stones and crystals, this will come as no surprise: It's often recommended that we drink crystal-infused water, to absorb the properties of crystals and infuse our body with the positive effects. Now, what is good for our bodies is usually good for our plants, too. So why not prepare crystal-infused water for your plants? Clean your stones and place them in a watering can or a carafe. Add water (purified or distilled water, or rainwater) and infuse for a minimum of three hours or overnight. Start with the basic combination of amethyst (harmonizing), rose quartz (cleansing), and clear quartz (invigorating). Other great stones for watering your plants are aquamarine (boosts growth), moonstones (enhances vitality), and polished hematites (energizing and grounding). You can also use crystal-infused water in your mister every now and then! Spritz that good energy around!

let the energy flow with plants

A thriving *Alocasia* reigns over this plant shelfie with a variety of potted plants in terra-cotta pots.

In this chapter we've seen how plants can physically enhance the energy in our homes by purifying the air we breathe. We've also seen the positive effect of combining plants and crystals to bring in the good vibes. Now let's have a look at plants that are said to be bearers of good energy themselves, and let's also think about the ideal placement of plants to let the energy in your home flow.

When we speak of positive energy in the home, we have in mind the principles of feng shui. Feng shui is an ancient Chinese system of rules that govern spatial arrangement and orientation in relation to the flow of energy. Plants can contribute to the level of positive energy in many ways. They can balance the water element (one of feng shui's five elements; see page 57), bring fortune or luck, counteract negative forces, and bring a piece of nature indoors. Using the right plants can help balance energy levels in your home and contribute to a more wholesome living environment.

If you want to boost the positive energy in the space where you live, add one or a few of the following plants:

JADE PLANT (CRASSULA OVATA)

This hardy succulent, it's claimed, supports the luck of its owners. The fleshy, round leaves symbolize good fortune, and the plant is best placed in areas of the home connected to money and success. So how about adding a jade plant to your home office?

LUCKY BAMBOO (DRACAENA SANDERIANA)

In feng shui practice, this plant is considered the most favorable when it comes to good energy. Lucky bamboo activates stagnant energy and enhances the flow of positive energy throughout the home. The lucky bamboo can go literally anywhere in your space!

ORCHIDS

In feng shui, orchids are connected to serenity and love. They help improve relationships, promote peace, and enhance a serene atmosphere. Orchids are best placed in the relationship corners of your home (those areas where we tend to be closer to our significant other)—one ideal place is the bedroom (see page 214) but it can also be near the sofa or the tub, basically anywhere you live out your relationship. And orchids come in a huge variety. So if you're not a big fan of the common *Phalaenopsis* orchids (which can be found in most supermarkets), opt for a more exotic beauty like a *Cymbidium* orchid.

BOSTON FERN (NEPHROLEPIS EXALTATA)

The Boston fern is considered a welcoming plant. It is best placed in your entrance area or home office. This lush plant is also one of the best natural air purifiers, making it a true good-energy plant for every home!

MONEY TREE (PACHIRA AQUATICA)

Like the jade plant, the money tree is believed to enhance abundance and prosperity. Add one to your living room or home office for an uplifting effect on your work and creativity.

HERBS SUCH AS BASIL, ROSEMARY, AND THYME

These fragrant plants will bring positivity into your home in an instant. The aroma infuses rooms and heightens our sense of smell. They are believed to bring good energy into the home and are a perfect addition to kitchens.

According to feng shui, any plant that is vibrant, lush, and healthy will bring good energy—so the most important principle is to keep your plants happy and healthy. Whatever plant is dear to your heart and gives you a good feeling is the right plant for your home. Principles and rules are one thing, but nothing beats your intuition and feelings. So go for what makes you feel good, happy, and invigorated!

When it comes to the ideal placement of plants, the first and foremost rule is to listen to your intuition. Decorate your home with plants in the way that you like and that suits your personal style. In general, the addition of plants positively impacts our mental and physical health; they are beneficial for our creativity and help us unwind and focus.

Another rule concerns the growing conditions in your home. The levels of light, temperature, and humidity should always be considered when deciding on plant placement.

The principles of feng shui add another dimension when it comes to determining the placement of plants. Plants are used to attract love, to increase learning abilities and prosperity, and to improve overall luck. The principles work based on the *bagua* areas of your home, defined by the five elements (wood, fire, earth, metal, and water). Plants are part of the wood element and thus ideal for the east, southeast, and south *bagua* areas of your home. The north area should have only a few plants. But here again, we believe in the power of your plant-loving intuition; wherever you feel plants are thriving and happy, and making you happy, that's where you should place them!

opposite, top left: The jewel orchid, also known as *Ludisia discolor*, is an easygoing beauty, with its stunning foliage and delicate white blooms.

opposite, top right: Grow fragrant herbs, like rosemary, thyme, or lavender, in the windowsill and serve yourself before any meal.

opposite, bottom right: Like lucky bamboo, most *Dracaena* are very easygoing. Prune their canes (the stems of a *Dracaena*) and new foliage will sprout just below the cut in a few weeks. Propagate the removed cane for another plant.

opposite, bottom left: *Crassula ovata*, commonly known as jade plant, lucky plant, or money plant, is a succulent plant, native to South Africa and Mozambique.

plant tribe stories . . .
Michell Lott

"I learned to care for myself thanks to my plants."

Location

São Paulo, Brazil

Profession

Journalist, set designer

Zodiac

Sagittarius

Lives with

Partner Felipe and friends Júlia and Renata

Apartment size

968 square feet / 90 square meters

Favorite plant

Euphorbia cotinifolia

Plant decor idea

If you have too little light for plants to thrive, use dried plants to create a forest or savanna-style jungle, and don't be afraid to celebrate the different life stages of plants. For brightly lit areas, opt for dramatic colors and experimental arrangements. The more dramatic your interior design, the more outstanding your plants should be!

Number of plants

55

Instagram

@lottlott @efirocha @julia.anadam @renatamiwa

below, left: The patio garden features an array of extraordinary plants in any color but green.

bottom, left: The green and botanical vibe in Michell and Felipe's bedroom, even without plants.

below, right: Welcome to the cosmic spiritual retreat house of Michell Lott.

bottom, right: Michell believes we should celebrate all the stages of the plant cycle—noting that even dried plants can be a wonderful addition to a room.

There are homes with beautiful interiors, there also are homes with artistic interiors, and then there are homes that are art themselves. One of those is the São Paulo home of journalist and set designer Michell Lott. Hidden in a courtyard in the trendy Pinheiros district is the Casinha do Retiro Espiritual Cósmico, which translates to something like the cosmic spiritual retreat house. And the cosmic energy is palpable.

Michell Lott is truly a creative soul. You can see it from the moment he opens the door: His aura sparkles, he is both charming and inviting, as well as mysterious and intriguing—and his warm and cheerful Brazilian soul shines through it all. And not only his—he shares this amazing home with his partner, the musician and model Felipe Rocha, as well as creatives Júlia Anadam and Renata Miwa.

Michell's work as a set designer has a strong impact on the way he lives. "Having plants is something that connects to my work as a set designer; some of my plants were part of my set designs and I brought them back home. For me, plants are also a way to connect to myself and to nature again—especially in a big city like São Paulo." This philosophy is reflected in every corner of the house. The entrance lounge, which is too dark for houseplants, is painted a beautiful terra-cotta hue and hosts a fantastic savanna of dried plants and flowers.

Just off the kitchen, which is a visual explosion of radiant red and fluorescent yellow hues, lies perhaps the most colorful urban jungle in São Paulo—the courtyard garden. Enclosed by deep purple walls and boasting a collection of Michell's favorite plants, it includes *Euphorbia cotinifolia* as a highlight plant, several varieties of dark philo-

dendron, plus begonias, *Coleus*, and bunches of dried flowers, too.

The upper floors continue the lush sweep of color, with bedrooms painted in dusky pink, mustard yellow, and deep green.

Plants can be found in every room, but the outdoor courtyard reigns supreme as the main gathering spot and favorite place to relax, reflect, celebrate, and discuss new ideas and projects. Moreover, it is a strong connection to nature. "Being with plants helps [us] to connect to ourselves again. Also they make every place prettier," concludes Michell with a whimsical smile.

below: A colorful *Stromanthe triostar* matches the vibrant palette of Michell's kitchen.

plant tribe stories . . .
Ben Mayer

"I am a gardener at heart.
Plants have always been my friends."

Location

Munich, Germany

Profession

Hair and makeup artist

Zodiac

Virgo

Lives with

Solo

Apartment size

647 square feet / 60 square meters

Favorite plant

Philodendron gloriosum

Plant decor idea

Make your own handmade ceramic hanging
pots and fill them with trailing plants
to create a vertical jungle.

Number of plants

138

Instagram

@_neon_beige_

below, left: The open kitchen is framed by various plants such as spider plants, *Monstera acuminata,* and *Anthurium clarinervium.*

bottom, left: A *Pseudorhipsalis ramulosa* adds color to the moody apartment.

below, right: The asparagus fern enjoys the bright indirect light in Ben's living room.

bottom, right: Ben's bedroom features a plant shelf that functions as a plant nursery, too.

Munich is a picturesque and serene city in the south of Germany. It features abundant greenways, parks, and an alpine river flowing through the city center. It is also home to a space that any plant fan would love: the eclectic, moody, and very personal apartment of freelance hair and makeup artist Ben Mayer.

The Bavarian native grew up surrounded by gardens and forests, so he is deeply connected to plants and nature. As a kid, he collected stones, shells, and botanicals, and his passion and interest in all three has never ceased. Today, he runs a garden allotment not far from his city apartment and dedicates his free time to making pottery.

Ben's apartment is a thriving urban jungle and a genuine treasure trove. Handmade ceramics—planters, mugs, plates—are scattered everywhere, crystals large and small are dotted between the plants, shells and fossils are beautifully displayed, and a big feature wall holds a collection of framed butterflies (see page 63). Kilim rugs from a trip to Morocco add color to the moody, gray walls and vintage furniture.

"I have always been interested in gardening and plants. As a kid, I wanted to become a gardener or florist. I have always had plants, but I admit right now I have more than ever before. I am a collector—always on the hunt for new plants and objects," says Ben. "I started pottery to create ceramic pieces that suit my needs and my style—especially for plant pots." Natural objects like crystals and shells also play a key role in his style. "I like to believe they bring positive vibes into my home and life," he concludes.

below: Making notes of the evolution of your plants can help deepen your knowledge of your green friends.

bottom: Thriving plants wherever you look bring everything to life.

plant tribe stories . . .

Derek Fernandes

"You can definitely live with plants and pets together!"

Location

São Paulo, Brazil

Profession

Architect

Zodiac

Aquarius

Lives with

Cat Baunilha

Apartment size

861 square feet / 80 square meters

Favorite plant

Philodendron erubescens

Plant decor idea

Create a floating shelf above a table.

Number of plants

Approximately 50

Instagram

@derekfernandes @vanillaeamigos

Diffused light flows throughout the stylish São Paulo home of architect Derek Fernandes. The shadows of a tall *Strelitzia* play on the anthracite wall in the living room, creating a dramatic countereffect to the light-flooded, soft pink dining nook. Baunilha (Portuguese for vanilla) struts through the room, her fluffy, light fur making her the perfect hue for this apartment. Every detail reveals Derek's impeccable aesthetic. As an architect he understands proportion, but as a vintage furniture lover he also knows that accessories, colors, and textures bring magic to a space.

Derek's attachment to plants has somewhat unusual beginnings: After a breakup led him to a new home, he discovered how well houseplants can soothe the spirit. In his new place, Derek began dedicating more time and care to his plants, nurturing them into a little jungle. Caring for plants helped Derek rediscover happiness in his daily life and lifted him out of an emotional low.

Today his home is filled with more than fifty plants, some on a tiny balcony outside the bedroom, many on display in amazing plant installations he builds himself, like the floating jungle above the dining table.

Interestingly, nearly all the plants in his home were given to him, which simply reminds us: Sometimes a plant is the most beautiful and meaningful gift you can offer a friend!

opposite, top left: The tiny bedroom balcony functions as a plant hospital for infested plants.

opposite, bottom left: A handmade floating shelf with integrated designer lighting creates a wonderful plant shelf without taking any precious floor space.

opposite, right: Retro vibes in Derek's kitchen.

above: The *Philodendron* 'Red Emerald' thrives in the soft glow of Derek's pink dining room.

chapter 3

HAPPINESS WITH PLANTS

Aren't we all striving for more happiness in our lives? That intense feeling of joy, contentment, pleasure, or satisfaction. But what is happiness, in fact? And how do we reach a higher level of happiness in our everyday lives, which sometimes feel like a roller-coaster ride? People have agonized over this question for centuries. Psychologists have found that the key to happiness is the experience of positive emotions. In this chapter we'll look into the power of plants, your green buddies, to bring you happiness through the daily experience of positive emotions with them.

Happy people are not born that way. As many psychologists suggest, the difference between someone who is happy and someone who is not lies in the frequency and intensity of the experience of positive emotions. This does not mean that happy people never experience negative emotions. They just process negative emotions in a different way. We want to focus on positive emotions, however, and on how to increase their frequency in our lives. If you are holding this book in your hands, it will come as no surprise when we tell you, yes, plants can and will bring more happiness to your life! Let's have a look at how houseplants contribute to positive emotions.

The happy "cosmic family" of Michell Lott. He shares his apartment with his partner Felipe and creatives Júlia and Renata in the Pinheiros district of São Paulo.

above: A begonia in full bloom.

right: A young *Monstera deliciosa*. With age, more fenestrations in the new leaves appear, which adds to the charm of these monster plants.

opposite: Step in to the urban jungle of São Paulo barista Toy Taniel (see page 32). Nature and plants inspire happiness, even if the jungle is located on a patio.

keeping your plants happy

A blooming cactus is like a gift: The show lasts only a few hours or days, so enjoy it while you can.

Imagine the following scenario: You come home and—as a member of the Plant Tribe—the first thing you do is check on your plants. But what is this? Your *Calathea* has brown tips again—oh, and the rubber tree lost two more leaves. And your peace lily looks like it's gone through turmoil and riot. Your plants are clearly not happy. Does that make you happy? We doubt it! You feel your stress level rising. You experience anxiety—will you lose one of your plants for good? Now imagine this: You come home, and you check on your beloved plants. The fiddle-leaf fig is brimming with health and its shiny leaves seem to greet you. Your *Monstera* is unfurling yet another mature leaf with prodigious fenestrations. Oh, and the *Pilea* has even more babies! We can see your face—a smile from ear to ear—and the waves of joy and excitement rushing through your body. This is sheer happiness brought to you by your plants. The mere sight of happy and healthy plants that you care for triggers these positive emotions. And here is the simple key: Happy plants create happy owners!

The reward after caring for your green buddies: taking a break and relaxing like a royal.

plant care routines for more happiness

Take a moment in your day to take care of your plants, and yourself.

Happy plants need proper care. But caring for plants should not be yet another chore on your never-ending to-do list. Instead, consider it a chance to take your own time-out, a special and dedicated moment for both your plants and your soul.

Many plant books describe how to properly care for all kinds of houseplants. So, instead of repeating information, here we'll highlight a few simple ideas, some commonsense advice and basics, plus a few rituals to add happiness to your plant care routine.

A
MORNING
PLANT CARE RITUAL

B
WEEKLY
TIME-OUT RITUAL

C
SUNDAY-NIGHT
POOL PARTY

Start your day with a quiet moment in the company of your plants. Have your coffee, tea, or even breakfast quietly with your plants. Slowly welcome a new day of opportunities and changes, because life is in constant flux. Observe the changes in your plants and embrace the changes in your life. This will be beneficial for your plants, too, as they will enjoy the daily moment of your presence (see chapter 1).

Dedicate a specific time slot to your weekly plant care. This can be just ten minutes or even an hour, depending on the number of plants you have. Embrace the plant care as a time-out for yourself, too. Play your favorite music or take some extra time to meditate, or even do a few yoga poses before or after the plant care. Choose something that will help you feel better and reinvigorated. You'll see—plant care will become your favorite moment of the week!

Whether it's Sunday night or another night is up to you. But the idea remains the same: Throw a pool party for your plants! Well, not literally (though feel free to prepare a cocktail for yourself, if you wish). Take all your easily movable plants to the bathroom and give them a gentle shower. This will be a real treat for your plants! Not only will they get hydrated, they'll also get rid of the layers of dust and dirt in one go. Design the pool party to your liking—add a disco ball, strings of lights, or funky music—you're the party master!

happiness with plants

81

the foundations of happy plants

Light, water, soil, and love are the foundations of happy plants.

The highest priority for plants is light. More than water or fertilizer, a plant needs light. Not the light emitted by regular light bulbs but real, natural sunlight. Unlike animals, plants are able to make their own food through the chemical process of photosynthesis: A plant takes carbon dioxide from the air, water from the ground, and light from the sun, and converts them into carbohydrates and oxygen. The carbohydrates are used for plant growth, and the oxygen is released into the atmosphere. The oxygen that comes out is cleaner than what plants take in: They literally clean the air. Studies have shown that during this process some plants actually absorb toxins from the air and thus purify the oxygen that we breathe in. Without energy from light, a plant dies: It just stores the water that it takes from the soil in its leaves' cells until they burst or drown. And without the carbohydrates it obtains via photosynthesis, it won't be able to grow bigger. Giving your plant fertilizer won't do anything for it, either. Conclusion: Good plant parents make sure their plants have light. Water and the right soil come second, followed by pest control, fertilizer, proper temperature, humidity, and especially care and love.

But how do we know if a plant is getting the correct amount of light? You'll notice that most tropical houseplants grow well in so-called bright indirect light. This means approximately five to six hours of full light, usually near a window or skylight, but does not mean intense, direct sun—which can burn foliage. It is important to understand that natural light coming through a window is not as strong as the sunlight outside or even at a plant nursery. The intensity of light drops rapidly as you move away from the window: Moving a plant just two or three feet (half a meter to a meter) into the room can reduce the light it receives by more than 50 percent! This isn't always easy to see; even if a room looks bright in all corners, the actual light intensity may be fairly low. It is helpful to use a light meter, or a free light meter app on your phone, to make sure. Depending on the type of meter, the intensity of light will be measured in lux or foot-candles. Try measuring at different times of the day to see the range of light in each room.

- 500–2,500 lux, or 50–250 foot-candles, is low light.

- 2,500–10,000 lux, or 250–1,000 foot-candles, is low to medium light.

- 10,000–20,000 lux, or 1,000–2,000 foot-candles, is medium to bright indirect light.

- 20,000–50,000 lux, or 2,000–5,000 foot-candles, is bright direct sunlight.

previous page: Instead of
exposing an ugly grow light
bulb, screw it into your
designer light fixture for
a stylish look.

below, left: The grow
lights give the entire
bedroom a warm glow and
allow the plants to thrive
despite the lack of natural
light in this corner.

below, right: To grow
plants in the darkest
corner of a bedroom, Plant
Tribe member Jennifer
attached flat-panel grow
lights to the ceilings of
wine crates.

Did you know that plants said to thrive in low-light conditions are often plants that would do better in a spot with more light? Because they are tough and sturdy, they look OK and don't immediately die when placed in a shady corner. It's a good idea to rotate "low-light" plants to a brighter spot for a light boost every once in a while. When moving your plants to provide better light conditions, try to avoid big transitions: Going from shade to six hours of bright indirect light can be stressful for a plant—and placing it in a spot with direct sun may even cause sunburn! Better to move plants gradually, a few feet (one meter) at a time. The same rule applies to nurturing symmetrical plants. During its growth phase, a plant will turn its leaves to the light source, lean toward the light, and eventually bend. Asymmetry gives a plant a bit of character, but if you prefer stronger, more balanced plants, rotate the pots ninety degrees every time you water.

Directly or indirectly, water affects all facets of life. Without it, the earth would look nothing like it does today. Because water is a precious resource, sustainability and conservation are increasingly important. As plant parents, we can make a small contribution: When possible, water your house-plants with rainwater, or use a container to collect the first cold liters of water when you're getting a shower or bath up to temperature.

Just as plants need proper light, the right amount of water provides structural support, cools the plant down, and moves minerals to all the right places. When you buy a new plant, it may come with a tag showing a sun and a few water droplets—to indicate light and water requirements. Or the salesperson at the plant shop may simply tell you to water once a week. Proper watering, however, is not an exact science; it's something you learn by doing. The plant tag instructions can help you get an idea of what a plant likes: evenly moist soil, partially dry soil, or almost completely dry soil. Test how dry the soil is by using your fingers to check for moisture at least 2 inches (5 cm) below the surface.

It's important that the water actually reaches the roots of the plant. When soil is very dry, it is often compacted and pulling away from the edges of the pot. If you pour in some water, it will almost immediately flow along the edges and straight into the drainage hole at the bottom. Sometimes you think you watered correctly, but if water doesn't reach all the roots, they'll dry out and die. Aerating dry soil before watering is crucial if you want to prevent this. Use a plant stake or chopstick to delicately poke some aeration holes into the soil surface: This will eliminate dry pockets and allow you to water your plant evenly.

A freshly watered banana plant in the garden.

left: The best way to
water your plants? With
rain—if you have an
outdoor garden like this
one, then let a summer
shower work its magic
and refresh your plants.

below: Invest in a
beautiful watering can
that looks great in your
decor and feels good in
your hands.

The more light a plant receives, both in intensity and in duration, the more water is consumed during the process of photosynthesis. Which means that if your plant resides in a darker area of a room, it requires less water than a plant on a windowsill. Size also dictates how much water a plant needs. Small potted plants will dry out faster than large ones. Keep in mind that the soil of a plant is like a sponge: The amount of water it can contain is finite. Rewatering when the soil is still at its maximum saturation isn't a good idea and can cause root rot. Give the roots time to absorb the water you're giving them, and water again when the soil is partially dry (depending on your plant's needs). Some plants, like ferns or devil's ivy, will actually tell you when they're thirsty: The cells in their leaves are like water balloons, and when they're filled, the leaves become stiff and the plant stands upright. When there's not enough water, the balloon-like cells deflate and the plant looks wilted. Give it a nice sip of water and the plant will look happy again in no time.

The best water for your houseplants is room-temperature water. You can collect rainwater or snow to water your plants, as long as you make sure to use containers that are clean, so that they don't transfer any additives to the water you collect. Most of us use tap water to water our plants, however, which is totally fine if your tap water is of good quality. Ideally, let the water sit overnight, so that chlorine and fluoride can evaporate.

Watering plants should be a joyful activity instead of a chore. Invest in a nice watering can that's easy to handle and easy on the eyes. Since you'll be using this tool regularly, it'll be more enjoyable if you can leave it among your plants and don't need to put it away because of its looks.

Cacti, like this *Opuntia*, need a bright spot on the windowsill to soak up direct sunlight.

Dirty fingernails are a common side effect of being a happy Plant Tribe member. Unless you're growing plants in water or semi-hydroponically, soil or dirt or compost is part of your life in some way. Soil is where the roots find water and nutrients for growth, and it supports the leaves, stems, and branches aboveground. Potting mixes formulated for houseplants aren't the same as outdoor soil, which is composed primarily of clay, sand, and silt, and is heavy and tends to harden and dry out. Not ideal for a houseplant whose root system needs good air circulation! That's why most generic potting mixes contain peat moss or coconut fiber, along with perlite and compost: They're lightweight, with excellent water retention and drainage capacities. You can experiment with wood chips, peat moss, vermiculite, and sand to create your own personal recipe, but most ready-to-use mixes available in your local plant shop or garden center will suffice.

Different plants prefer different ingredients in their potting mixes. Succulents, cacti, and snake plants, for example, appreciate a porous medium with perlite, which allows water to run through quickly and dry up fast, whereas ferns thrive in a potting mix with peat moss, which helps the soil stay moist.

Fresh soil means new nutrients. Over time, soil runs out of essential nutrients, and for this reason alone plants typically need to be repotted every twelve to eighteen months. If your plants are doing well, they may outgrow their pots even more quickly, showing signs of roots poking through the drainage holes at the bottom of the pots or pushing the plant out of the planter. Watch for these other telltale signs, too: top-heavy plants that threaten to fall over, slower than usual growth of your plants, salt and mineral buildup on the plant or pot, and plants that dry out easily and require frequent waterings (usually because there's not enough soil to contain the water). If you see any of these, then it's time to repot!

When you want to repot your houseplant, make sure the new planter is no more than 2 inches (5 cm) wider than the old pot for plants up to 10 inches (25 cm) tall, or no more than 4 inches (10 cm) wider for bigger plants. Moving a plant into a pot that is too big will slow down its growth, as it will spend most of its energy growing roots instead of new foliage. With an oversize pot you'll also run the risk of giving your plant too much water and thus increase the chances of root rot.

Early spring, before the start of the growth season, is the best time to repot houseplants. Repotting usually means additional stress for a plant, so keep an eye on your green buddy in the weeks after repotting and make sure it's adapting to the new pot and potting mix.

Early spring, before
the start of the growth
season, is the best time
to repot houseplants.

PESTS

Living with plants means living with the bugs who eat and make their homes in them. Having bugs in your plants is natural. Even if you've been pest-free so far, chances are that sooner or later you'll face some houseplant bugs. Dealing with sick or infested plants can be frustrating, nerve-racking, disgusting, or even scary, but it's a responsibility we assume in caring for a living creature. Just like humans, plants treated for illness need time to recover.

To keep pests to a minimum, start at the beginning. When adding a new plant to your home, inspect before you buy. Touch and feel the leaves, check for bugs between and under them and in the soil. If there are no rotten leaves or suspicious spots on the leaves, go ahead and adopt that beauty. If you discover pests on a plant in a shop or nursery, tell the owner, so that the plant can be quarantined and not be sold to anyone else. Even if you examine a plant really closely, you may not see future pests. Eggs in the soil are hard to spot, and sometimes you don't notice something is wrong until it's too late. Always use clean pots and potting soil when repotting newly adopted plants, and remove any potential pests from the soil ball around the plant. To be on the safe side, isolate the new plant from your other plants for a few days and check the leaves and stems every day. Using a magnifying glass can help you identify the start of an outbreak. When you think all is good, move the plant to its intended spot. Inspect it carefully on a regular basis, for example, when you water it.

Here are some of the most common pests and ways to deal with them.

above: A common nuisance for plant lovers: fungus gnats. Neem oil or yellow sticky traps are great ways to get rid of them.

left: This agave suffered a serious mealybug attack. The owner separates infested plants in a quarantine area on his small balcony and treats them there.

FUNGUS GNATS

It's not the fungus gnats but their larvae that do the damage. The annoying black flies that swarm around your plants lay eggs in the plant soil, and the larvae eat soil fungi and fresh new roots. This weakens the plant and can make it look pale and droopy. Fungus gnats love moist compost, so the first thing to do if you spot them is to let the soil of your plant dry out as much as you can without killing your plant.

In the meantime, set up a trap to catch the gnats by filling a small glass with apple cider vinegar and a few drops of dish soap. Cover the top with packing tape and punch several small openings in it, so that the flies can get in but not out. For maximum effect, add some yellow sticky traps around your plants to attract hovering adults.

Another remedy is to cover the soil in the pot with a layer of sand or small pebbles. The gnats lay their eggs in the top ¼ inch (0.5 cm) of moist soil. If you top the soil with ¼ to ½ inch (0.5 to 1 cm) of sand, it'll drain quickly, which can confuse the gnats into thinking the soil is dry. You can use colorful decorative sand to have fun!

If nothing else works, water your plants with a mixture of one part 3-percent hydrogen peroxide and four parts water. The peroxide will kill any eggs or larvae, and it also oxygenates the soil and flushes out other bacteria and fungal growth, making your plants extra happy and healthy. Repeat the treatment a few times to catch any newly laid eggs.

SPIDER MITES

These arachnids are very small and hard to see, and you most often realize your plant is infested only when the mites have already invaded. They leave your plants speckled or pinpricked, sometimes wilting, and give them an ugly bronze color. Spider mites like direct sunlight and thrive in hot, dry conditions—in the middle of the summer, for example, or in winter's dry indoor heat.

To get rid of these pests, wipe away as many mites and webs as possible and then spray with insecticidal soap or a horticultural oil like organic neem oil. Repeat weekly for a few weeks to eliminate any new mites. Make sure to cover the soil before treating your plant, so the mites don't fall back into the soil.

MEALYBUGS

Mealybugs are some of the messiest pests because their white cotton-like fluff is so sticky. These tiny unarmored scale insects, which feed on plant juices and also transmit several plant diseases, produce a white protective powder to nest in, and this fuzzy coating also protects them from water and pesticides. They like to nest between branches or leaves, or on the undersides of leaves, so the only way to remove them is by hand, one by one, with a Q-tip dipped in rubbing alcohol. Heavy infestations can also be controlled with insecticidal soap or organic neem oil. If you have a garden or balcony, during the warmer season you can let nature—specifically, ladybugs, lacewings, and syrphid flies—do what it does best: Eat the mealybugs!

left: If you have no special
treatments in the house and
you discover thrips on your
plants, use some alcohol.
Here, a cloth dipped in vodka
does the job.

opposite: An infested
Thaumatophyllum xanadu
receives careful treatment.

THRIPS

When you see that your plant isn't doing well, even though you didn't change its location or the surrounding temperature, or spoil it with too much fertilizer, it's likely your plant is being attacked by thrips. Thrips are hard to see without a magnifying glass, and when you do see them, the damage has already been done. These black or brown miniature winged insects suck the juices out of leaves and stems, causing them to become dry and unpleasantly rubbery. The larvae can be green or yellow. Before you notice a thrips invasion, you may see tiny black spots on your plant's leaves: It's the bugs' poop. Be warned, and start treating your plant before it's too late.

To treat, first shower the plant with water, then use an insecticidal soap or organic neem oil on all sides of the plant, and repeat weekly for three weeks. Adult thrips are attracted to the color blue, so you can also use sticky blue tape around your pots to trap them.

SCALE

These common indoor pests, which thrive in warm and dry environments, have flat, oval, beige or brown shells. They suck the sap from your plant, which can leave it yellowing and wilting. Generally slow movers, hard scale insects find plants with bark or a really thick protective layer too much work to infest. But they love stiff, fleshy, juicy plants like snake plants, cacti, succulents, and bird's-nest ferns.

When they feed, the bugs secrete a sweet, sticky substance called honeydew that makes your plant's leaves and your shelf or tabletop sticky. To get rid of these pests, remove the honeydew with a cloth and some mild liquid soap. There are two types of scale: hard and soft. The latter can be treated by spraying, but the hard ones have tougher shells and thus they are not as easy to eradicate. Scrape the insects off the leaves with the blunt side of a knife, your fingernail, or a toothpick. Or use a Q-tip dipped in rubbing alcohol and remove them one by one. Then spray weekly with organic neem oil.

happiness with plants

Keep your plants
happy and thriving
by treating them
with love, respect,
and good care.
Always opt for
organic solutions
and feed them
during their growth
period.

Many chemical pesticides are highly toxic and will damage a plant faster than any colony of bugs. Besides, most pesticides aren't meant for use on houseplants, require a well-ventilated space, and are harmful to the environment as well as to your health. Some chemical pesticides actually encourage the spread of pests by killing the beneficial insects that prey on them. Some pests, such as spider mites, quickly become resistant to various pesticides, which means it's easier to control them with effective natural and organic methods. When possible, find an alternative, more natural solution, like beneficial insects or organic neem oil, to get rid of pests on your plant.

First, let's get this myth out of the way: Fertilizer isn't "plant food," even though it's often called that. Fertilizer can be seen instead as a vitamin boost for your plants. The minerals in fertilizers replace nutrients that the soil will lose over time. While some plants enjoy a scoop of fresh nutrient-rich soil in their pot, or timely repotting, others grow faster and stronger with a regular dose of fertilizer. Plants need fertilizer only when they're growing and when they haven't recently been repotted. Fast-growing plants like peace lilies should be fertilized more often than slow growers like cacti, as they extract more nutrients from the soil to grow. Fertilizers come in many different forms, from slow-release pellets to synthetic liquids to organic powders. Because organic fertilizers contain decomposing organic matter, they, naturally, stink, but their natural ingredients make them milder than the chemical varieties. If you care about the planet and keeping your living space as healthy and natural as possible, you may want to get an organic, and stinky, fertilizer.

Any fertilizer you buy will come with information about the nutrients that it contains and its N–P–K ratio, the percentages of nitrogen (N), phosphorus (P), and potassium (K) in the product. Different ratios work for different plants, so check the needs of your houseplants before buying new fertilizer. When using fertilizer, keep in mind that in general it's better to under-fertilize than to over-fertilize: You don't get better results by giving your plants extra fertilizer. You even expose your plants to so-called fertilizer burn: The excess nutrients and salts basically burn the foliage, and the plant may die. Simply dilute your fertilizer slightly more than the instructions state, and you and your plant will be fine.

botanical joy

Even during difficult moments in life, joy can be a tool for coping with stress. It's a form of resilience. When we feel stressed, our bodies are flooded with chemicals like cortisol and epinephrine, which raise our heart rate and blood pressure, keep us alert and focused, and help us deal with the situation at hand. This automatic response works well when the stress is temporary, but if stress becomes chronic, it can lead to exhaustion and illness. By giving your body a break from this stress response, through a moment of pure joy, you enable it to recover. At the same time, you help yourself to recover mentally. Experiencing positive emotions like joy can break the pattern of sadness or anxiety, give you a new perspective, and help you connect with others and find happiness and increased well-being.

When we go through tough and stressful events, however, we're tempted to forgo joy and focus on the problem. We think we don't have enough time, money, or energy to spend on joy, and instead we keep to ourselves and wait for better things to come. Or we feel guilty about being joyful, as if it would be inappropriate to laugh or have a good time while others are suffering.

Now, there are plenty of things that produce joy in most of us, like the first spring blossoms, tree houses, or a beautiful rainbow. There's something about joy that may seem playful or frivolous, but ignore the judgmental voices and think about the big picture: When you're eighty years old, will you remember the time when you laughed until your belly ached because of a silly joke, or the moment when you decided not to wear a red hat because you were afraid of people staring at you?

While experiencing joy may seem superficial and silly, adding little touches of joy to your everyday life can have a huge impact on your overall feeling of happiness. It's simple and doesn't have to cost a lot.

opposite: Apollo's head is crowned by the *Phlebodium* blue star, a divinely beautiful fern.

above: Start the day full of joy, surrounded by your houseplants.

THREE RECIPES FOR BOTANICAL JOY

SMILEY FACE

Stick a pair of googly eyes on your planter or draw a smiley on a simple flower-pot. It will make you smile when you need it, and if you don't like it anymore, turn the pot around and no one will notice the happy face with cool green hair!

MAKE BOTANICAL CONFETTI

Use a hole punch to turn a few sturdy leaves (from cherry laurel shrubs, for example) into some green confetti. You can throw it around outside without worrying about your ecological footprint.

PLANT PORTRAIT

Gather all your plants in one place. Depending on the number of plants you have, this can be quite a task. Arrange them the way you would a family picture: the tallest ones in back, the kids in front. Take the picture, print it, and frame the portrait of your plant family.

If you want to feel happy, remember that comparing what you have with what others have will rob you of your joy. It's a cliché but so true. Your (and our!) wish list of plants gets longer every day. Seeing other plant people possessing all these beautiful plants and showing them off on social media can make us pretty jealous. We're happy for them, but oh boy, how we'd love to add that full-grown *Monstera deliciosa variegata* or that thriving rare aroid plant to our own homes. Instead of comparing our own plant gang to other people's plant collections, we prefer to focus on keeping our own plants as happy as possible. We may not have the most perfect collection of plants, but they are ours to care for. They bring us joy and happiness, grow with us over time, and, with their imperfect shapes, are just as unique as we are.

grow your own plants

Divided *Aloe* cuttings waiting to be potted.

Growing your own houseplants is one of the most rewarding things you can do. Seeing the process of germination—the growth of the roots and the emergence of the stem and the first leaves—is truly magical. Some plants, particularly avocados, mangoes, and palm trees, are very easy to grow from seeds. Once you know how to grow a plant from an avocado pit or mango seed, you won't be able to throw them away after making guacamole, avocado toast, or a mango smoothie. Let us show you how!

AVOCADO PLANT

There are several techniques for growing your own avocado plant. The most common is the toothpick method, in which you pierce the pit with tooth-picks, forming a scaffold to hold the pit partially submerged in water. We prefer dipping the entire avocado pit in water, and not scarring it. Wash and dry the pit, and carefully peel off the brown skin with a knife, without nicking the pit. Fill a glass, vase, or cup with water, almost to the brim. Put the pit in the water, broad end first, and keep it in place with a structure of washi tape or by using a ceramic propagation tray or a propagation cone (see page 181). Place the glass in a warm, sunny spot, but out of direct sunlight, and replace the water at least once a week. It can take a few weeks, or up to several months, for an avocado pit to germinate. And sometimes nothing happens. But if you're lucky, roots and a stem will appear, and soon the first leaves. When the roots have grown thick, you can transfer the avocado plant to a pot, leaving half the pit exposed above the soil. Water several times a week: Avocado plants are thirsty. To give your avocado plant a bushier look, pinch off the stem and it will grow new shoots. Don't expect your avocado plant to produce fruit immediately—that can take as long as twenty years—but consider it a fun experiment and a free houseplant!

An avocado propagation station with a variety of glass vessels and jars perfect for holding avocado pits.

MANGO PLANT

Enjoy eating your mango, and then cut away all the flesh from the husk at the center of the fruit. Carefully cut the husk open with a sharp knife and remove the flat, bean-shaped seed. Compost the husk. Wrap the seed in a damp paper towel and put it in a zip-top bag, and place the bag on a warm, sunny windowsill. Then wait for the seed to sprout, which can take a couple of weeks. When there are roots and a few leaves, you can pot up your baby mango plant. Be sure to give it full sun and lots of water. And there you have it: another free home-grown houseplant!

PALM TREE

Be aware that growing a palm tree from seed is a long process, but the results are worth it. Start by finding a flowering palm tree, and look up to see if you can spot any seeds on the branching fluo-rescences. The seeds' appearance and color vary depending on the species: Some are small and red, while others are bright green or just turned yellow. If the seeds in the palm tree are out of reach, look on the ground. Take the fresh seeds home and test whether they're viable by dropping them into a bowl of warm water. Any seeds that float are unlikely to sprout and can be discarded. Next, gently peel off the skins of the remaining seeds, if possible; if not, leave them as they are and plant them in some soil. Keep the newly planted seeds in a bright, warm spot and water regularly to keep the soil moist (but not soggy). The time till germination varies widely among palm species, but in general it's much longer than you'd expect. Some palm seeds will sprout in two months; others can easily take six months. Young palm seedlings can be repot-ted when they have at least three leaves. When growing your own palm tree, start with at least a dozen seeds: Uncover the seedlings from the soil throughout the process to admire the strength of the roots and first palm leaves. The small sprouting seeds are susceptible to root shock when you do this, but if you start with several dozen palm seeds, losing a few isn't so bad. It'll be years before you can lie in a hammock stretched between your own palm trees and sip a cocktail, but you can dream!

left: Palm fronds add an instant jungle vibe to any plant throne. Even though it is a long process, sometimes it is fun and worth the work to try growing palm trees from seeds collected during your last vacation.

opposite: A *Licuala grandis* and a *Livistona* share a sunny spot in the corner of a dining room.

Propagation Station

Vines like *Tradescantia zebrina* or *T. pallida*, pothos, and *Philodendron* are very easy to propagate in water: Simply cut a piece off the main stem of the mother plant and place it in a small vase filled with water, and there'll be roots in no time. Once they're 1 to 2 inches (2.5 to 5 cm) long, you can plant them in soil. Propagating these "easy" plants is a wonderful way to learn more about plant growth: Study the colors of the roots, and their sizes and structures, and watch how fast they grow—it's spectacular.

Succulents like jade plants or *Echeveria* varieties can be propagated by wiggling some leaves off the stem of a healthy adult plant. Lay the leaves flat on some soil spread in a small dish, or on top of the soil of a larger plant, and let them dry out—don't water immediately. After a few days, gently sprinkle water over the leaves. Water again once the soil is completely dry. You can water once every ten days, or even less. Like grown-up succulents, they don't need a lot of water. Place your leaves in a spot with lots of indirect sunlight. After a few weeks, miniature white or pink roots will sprout from the tips of the leaves, and a teeny-tiny baby plant will start to grow. Once your new succulents are a little bit bigger you'll notice that the original leaves have become wrinkly, yellow, or dry. Detach them carefully and plant the new succulents in their own pots.

Glass vases and domes turn into ideal propagation vessels.

share your plant happiness

A gift that keeps on giving . . . living! Like this gorgeous *Adenia glauca*.

Plant gifts are a wonderful idea to surprise your friends. It doesn't have to be a full-grown *Monstera* plant. Maybe a small *Tillandsia* or any other small potted plant will do the trick. Simply share your plant happiness with others!

Enjoying your thriving plants on your own is fantastic, but sharing your love for greenery with others gets you the gold (and green!) medal and doubles your plant happiness. If your partner, friends, or neighbors are not as enthusiastic about your plants as you are, share your passion with like-minded people: Find your Plant Tribe! When we founded Urban Jungle Bloggers we soon realized there are plant-loving people all around the world, and sharing our experiences with others has been a rewarding process. We learn so much from one another, whether we're professional plant doctors or plant hobbyists: There is knowledge in every corner of the globe. Different houseplants are popular in different places; keeping a plant healthy in a humid climate isn't the same as keeping it alive during a long, dark winter in the Northern Hemisphere. Exchanging knowledge—the best green-interior experiences, tips, and tricks—and sharing love for a planty home are at the heart of the Urban Jungle Bloggers community. You can find your tribe online, by using the hashtag #urbanjunglebloggers on Instagram. Tag your own botanical decor with the same hashtag, or mention @urbanjungleblog in your photos and stories. We love sharing inspiring homes and plants with all the members of our Urban Jungle Bloggers community. You may discover some new accounts, make new plant friends, or even join a botanical workshop.

PLANT GIFTS

Propagating and growing new plants is an ongoing process. Once you get the hang of it, it's likely you will have a few cuttings growing at all times. And what makes a nicer gift than a homegrown houseplant? Find a nice ceramic flowerpot, pot one of your baby plants in some fresh soil, give it a new name, write the plant's care instructions on a postcard, wrap a big ribbon around the pot, and gift it to a loved one. There you have it: a thoughtful green gift that won't break the bank.

Forget the bottle of wine—bring a small cutting or bigger *Monstera deliciosa* as a housewarming gift.

PLANT SWAPS

Once you've learned to successfully propagate your *Tradescantia*, *Pilea*, and spider plants, you may find you are up to your ears in plants of the same variety. A plant swap is the perfect way to thin out extra plants while scoring new ones to enjoy. It allows you to grow your urban jungle at limited cost and to socialize with fellow plant lovers. Many plant swaps start with an introduction, a talk on a plant-related subject, or a Q&A session on plant care, and are organized by botanical institutions, plant shops, plant enthusiasts, or *you*! Why not gather some friends, family, colleagues, and Instagram pals in a café or at someone's home and swap some plants? Or propose that a local community center host the event as a fundraiser, while you volunteer your time to help set it all up. Selling tickets at a nominal fee will ensure that people actually show up on the day of the swap, and proceeds can be used to cover the costs of the event space and refreshments, or be donated to a charity. Ask fellow plant swappers to label their healthy, pest-free plants and cuttings with their names, the names of the plants (if they know them), and where they come from. Additional information, such as care instructions or a plant anecdote, is nice, too. As the host, make sure to bring a supply of labels and markers as well as some extra plants, to ensure that no one leaves empty-handed. Keep it low-key, mingle with fellow plant lovers, and enjoy!

If you don't want to organize a plant swap but would like to participate, check town bulletins, local publications, social media groups or hashtags (#plantswapCITYNAME), or announcements on event-oriented sites and apps for the next swaps in your area.

above: Small potted baby plants are a wonderful gift for friends and family—whether it is a housewarming gift, a birthday present, or just a token of love and friendship.

opposite: Visiting a greenhouse can invigorate your body and soul.

When your plant friends don't live nearby, but you still want to surprise them with plant cuttings, did you know that you can send them easily via snail mail? Just make sure to check postal regulations first, since the rules vary by country and state. To send a small plant cutting to a friend, first wrap the roots (not the stem and leaves!) in some wet tissue paper, then place the wrapped roots inside a reusable ziplock bag or enclose them in beeswax paper. Use crumpled tissue to create a frame around the cutting (to protect it from being crushed in the mail) and then just slide it into an envelope. For larger cuttings, you can use a flat cardboard box that fits through the mail slot. Or go for a bigger box and add some extra fun stuff in the package, so the small cutting won't rattle around. Recycle boxes from previous packages: The box may be ugly, but it's what's inside that counts!

Most common cuttings will survive up to ten days with the water supply in the wet tissue paper and regenerate when they are put in water upon arrival. To lower the risk of your cutting drying out during its travel, use overnight or express shipping for your parcel. Also, make sure to send your plant gift in the warmer months both in your area and at its destination, to keep the cutting from freezing in cold distribution centers. When you know it's warm and sunny, you may want to write "no direct sunshine" on the outside of your package; if your mail carrier leaves it in the burning sun, the cutting can dry out fast.

Wandering around the well-maintained parks, lush humid greenhouses, or dry conservatories of a botanical garden is one of our favorite activities when we travel. Experiencing the greenery (especially while in the midst of a bustling city) creates a feeling of calm and belonging.

Botanical gardens are dedicated to the collection, cultivation, preservation, and display of a wide range of plants (all labeled with their scientific names). Some contain special plant collections, such as cacti and other succulents, herbs and plants with healing properties, or plants from specific parts of the world. What makes botanical gardens even more interesting and amazing is getting to see full-grown examples and "family members" of your everyday houseplants. Botanical gardens are a source of inspiration and knowledge, whether you are discovering new species, admiring rare plants, or simply appreciating a blooming beauty or the gracefulness of wilting leaves. Bring a friend for a walk around the garden, or plan a walking meeting with your coworkers or clients in a green environment. A change of scene will spark new ideas and bring new insights. And you won't be short on conversation: There's so much to see and discover together.

happiness with plants

living happily ever after with plants

A few mature plants can add an instant jungle vibe to any room.

Adopting a new plant from a plant shop, nursery, or garden center is only the beginning of your life together. It can be the start of several decades of greenery, or it may be that your married bliss won't stand the test of time.

Buying a new plant is not the same as buying a bouquet of cut flowers that will be gone in a week. Most of the houseplants that are for sale in plant shops and garden centers can live for years. Modern growers make sure conditions for their baby plants are excellent: They provide the perfect temperature, the correct exposure to indirect sunlight, enough water, and an extra dose of fertilizer to make the plants grow as quickly and healthily as possible. Growing plants is a business like any other, with greenhouses that consume electricity, water, and other natural resources. When you adopt your new plant, it will have traveled for many miles between different nurseries that attend to your plant's various growth stages, pruning, care, and packaging. Which makes it a consumer product the same as your breakfast cereal or dining room chair. Plants can teach you a lot about nature and growth, however. They create awareness and make you realize that life takes time, that growing healthy roots or blooming requires both resources and patience. These are key considerations no matter whether you are adopting a new plant or trying to live a more sustainable life and make better and healthier choices for yourself and your family.

When your new plant arrives in your home it will slowly adapt to the circumstances. Assuming you don't live in a greenhouse (and you are not a greenhouse robot that waters plants the second they need it), the light and temperature will be different. For the plant, this may be stressful at first, but if you provide it with suitable light and keep an eye on its development, it will probably do just fine. In its new home, your perfect plant will change: It will grow toward the light, and if you don't turn it around every now and then, it will bend toward that bright window. It will stretch to reach for more light, lose a few leaves, change color, and grow smaller leaves, or thrive and surprise you with new blooms, bigger leaves, new patterns, and offshoots. It will show you its true character and wear its scars with pride. Helping your plant grow older requires dedication and a healthy dose of TLC. It will bounce back after an invasion of pests, lose a few leaves whenever you move it, and suffer a bit if your plant sitter over-waters it during your vacation, but you and it will live and grow older. Together. There is something magical about mature houseplants: They look different and reveal their true character, and with that the character of their plant parent—you!

Plants and art are a striking combination. Here, a vintage painting peeks through a tall *Euphorbia trigona*.

HELP, MY PLANT GOT TOO BIG!

Even the smallest supermarket cacti are at least a few months old. Which explains the steep prices charged for mature plants, whose care—often over a few years—takes up space and uses resources. These plants are living beings that wait for their plant parent to give them a new life in a home with enough space for them to thrive. And someday your plant may even outgrow your home! What to do? If you don't want to cut it back or divide it into smaller plants, you may need to find your plant a new owner. In that case, offer it to a plant-loving friend, ask around on social media, or even check at a local plant shop that might be interested in adopting your green roommate. But if you are not ready to let go of your roomie, you can cut it back to a smaller size, use some leaves for propagation (they make great plant gifts!), or divide the plant with its roots into several medium-size plants. Big plants like rubber trees, *Monstera deliciosa*, or fiddle-leaf figs can easily be reduced in size by cutting the tallest branches off the top, just above a node. Always use a sharp and clean knife for pruning. After a few months, new branches will appear on the stem, just below where you cut it. Don't throw these cut-off branches away; place them in water to grow new roots. Once the roots are strong, you can pot them and you'll have a new houseplant!

opposite: The mature leaves of the *Anthurium veitchii* can reach the size of an adult human being. Just like us, they also show signs of age and maturity on their leaves. Embrace the beauty of mature plants!

right: Adopt healthy, mature plants to make a visual statement in your home. Here, Olive and Rudy (see page 148) add a mature *Ficus* and *Pilea* to their urban jungle in Dallas.

ADOPT A HEALTHY PLANT

When purchasing a new plant, make sure it is happy and bug-free. Feel the leaves, and check that there are no bugs between or under the leaves and in the soil. No rotten leaves or suspicious spots on the leaves? Then you are good to go! A little side note: Even if you examine a plant really closely, you may overlook some existing pests. Living with plants means that you'll occasionally live with plant pests. It's part of plant life and an interesting learning experience. See page 90 for our advice on pests. Also, as you transport your plant home, keep it away from cold and drafts. If the weather is really cold or hot and sunny, protect your plant with some blankets or recycled paper to keep it happy until you're home.

happiness with plants

113

above: The plants in the home of Plant Tribe members Tim and Hannes (see page 202) are mostly mature and big. Tim and Hannes love the lush jungle feeling created by the huge foliage, which also adds to their domestic happiness.

right: A mature *Strelitzia,* or bird-of-paradise, and a *Monstera deliciosa* snuggle in the dining room corner next to a wall with botanical plates.

WHERE DO I FIND OLDER MATURE PLANTS?

If you don't want to wait until your *Monstera* grows into a huge king of the jungle, you can try to source an older plant. While you may not find one in many plant shops, you can try your luck at any of these places:

- Plant shelters: Just as in animal shelters, passionate volunteers take care of plants that outgrew their previous owners' homes. This is also where you can bring your plants when you move across the country and can't take them with you.

- Online or local newspapers: Yes, you can find older plants online or in the newspaper! In exchange for a small (or, sometimes, large) fee, or a bottle of wine, you can pick up plants that someone wants to get rid of. It may be worth driving a few extra miles to find your dream plant.

- Social media groups or online forums: Connect with like-minded plant lovers and keep an eye out for ads with larger plants. Or post your own request.

- Garage sales and flea markets: Now that people are Marie-Kondo-ing their homes, you can adopt the plants that don't spark joy for them anymore!

- A downsizing friend: If a friend or relative is downsizing to a smaller home, they may have large plants (a mature jade plant, for example) that they can't fit in their new space.

- Your local plant shop or nursery: Ask if they can help you source an older plant.

WHAT DO I DO WHEN I FIND AN OLDER PLANT?

As with the purchase of a new plant, always check for bugs and pests. You don't want your new companion to spread disease to your other plants. In addition, when you adopt a mature plant, don't repot it immediately. Give it a few weeks, and check whether the roots need more space, or if the soil looks tired and needs to be renewed. If necessary, repot in adequate soil, ideally in spring or summer when the plant is active. Repeat every two to three years on average. And then get to know each other, see how you like each other. If it turns out you are not made for each other, you can always part ways. Giving away your old friend to a new plant parent who loves it makes three happy parties: your friend, your plant, and you. Win, win, win!

EASY OLDIES
(Plants That Easily
Grow to Maturity)

- Boston ferns (*Nephrolepis exaltata*)
- Jade plants (*Crassula ovata*)
- *Monstera deliciosa*
- Rubber plants (*Ficus elastica*)
- Christmas or Thanksgiving cacti (*Schlumbergera*)
- Snake plants (*Sansevieria*)
- Spider plants (*Chlorophytum comosum*)
- Weeping figs (*Ficus benjamina*)

left: A mature *Ficus alii*
bends toward the light.
Sometimes the odd shapes and
growth patterns are part of
a mature plant's charm.

opposite: These rare and
mature philodendrons and
anthuriums are part of
a large collection. The
biggest plants such as the
Philodendron esmeraldense
and *Philodendron spiritus-
sancti* sit on the owner's
small balcony, enjoying the
Brazilian climate.

plant potions for happy plants

Mix your own plant potion for happy, thriving plants.

WILLOW WATER

The bark of weeping willows contains salicylic (SA) and indolebutyric (IBA) acids, which contain natural plant growth hormones and can be used for rooting new cuttings. Collect some young twigs with green or yellow bark from any willow species. Remove the leaves and cut the twigs into 1-inch (2.5-cm) pieces and put them in a mason jar or bottle. Cover with unheated tap water and let them soak for three weeks. Both SA and IBA will leach into the water. The SA helps plants fight off infections and increases their chances of survival, while the IBA stimulates root growth. When the three weeks are up, remove the twigs from the water and compost them, and use the liquid to jump-start new cuttings. Soak the stems of the cuttings in the liquid for a few days (as if they were flowers in a vase) and prepare them as you would any other cuttings. Or water your new plant cuttings with the willow water to give them an extra boost and help them root!

SOIL AERATION

If you want to "do something" for your plant, but you know it has already had enough to drink, why not aerate the soil? In nature, earthworms and other insects do their thing and loosen the soil around a plant so that oxygen can get to the roots and rainwater moistens the soil evenly. Since our houseplants lack earthworms, it's important to aerate the soil by hand to keep its structure in balance. When you water your plants from the top, the soil will become more compact over time. To aerate the soil, you can delicately poke a chopstick or plant stake into it. Inevitably, you will break some roots, but they'll grow back; soil compaction will kill many more by suffocation. Aerate the soil before watering your plants to allow the water to run through more easily.

Homemade willow water will give a boost to your cuttings, like this neon pothos in Julie Hagan's home.

Juliette Becquart

"Life with a baby turned out much greener than I expected!"

Location

Fontenay-sous-Bois, France

Profession

Photographer, blogger

Zodiac

Virgo

Lives with

Husband Gaëtan, son Louison, cat Sherlock

Apartment size

860 square feet / 80 square meters

Favorite plant

Alocasia reginula 'Black Velvet'

Plant decor idea

Small plant "shelfies" displayed against a colorful wall.

Number of plants

50

Instagram

@juliette_jnspc @gaetan

When Juliette and Gaëtan moved into their new home in the suburbs of Paris, they owned a single plant: an aloe in a terrarium. Although they always liked the idea of having plants at home, they didn't really know where to start. This changed when Juliette worked on a blog project focused on decorating a home with greenery. She collaborated with local plant shops, chose plants and ceramics (by Camille & Clémentine, Mimi Ceramics by Mica DeMarquez, and Studio Arhoj), and installed them on randomly spaced wall shelves. She named these "plant shelfies" and her current collection now dresses up a formerly empty living room wall. "Immediately after we installed the plants, our home felt so fresh! The big Boston ferns helped improve the quality of the air and we truly felt it. I'm spending more time at home now with our son, Louison, and I spend my days caring for him as well as our collection of plants. It is actually addictive: Instead of buying more art books and comics, we now buy new plants."

Plant care is a daily ritual: With Louison on one hip and a mister in hand, Juliette mists and prunes where needed and likes to tell her son about the *Stromanthe triostar* and the staghorn ferns. "For now, he prefers playing with the spray bottle itself, but I can't wait for us to take care of our greenery together. I'm happy to be able to teach him more about plants in a few years."

In just a short period of time, plants have become an important part of life in this cozy and bright home. "Plants bring so much happiness that we don't think twice when looking for a housewarming gift for our friends or a birthday gift for a family member: We choose a nice plant and find a matching ceramic pot. Everyone loves it!"

opposite: With the arrival of baby Louison, plants moved into the Paris home of Juliette, too.

top: The blue feature wall is a perfect backdrop for the display of plants.

above: A *Ficus elastica* sits in the corner of Juliette's colorful living room.

Rebecca Breach

"I want everyone to love plants as much
as I do: I love to give them as gifts—
to share the texture of the soil, the scent
of the leaves, the sense of nature."

Location

Paris, France

Profession

Urban gardener at Jardinière Sauvage

Zodiac

Libra

Lives with

Son Aleksi

Apartment size

1,180 square feet / 110 square meters

Favorite plant

Tomato plants

Plant decor idea

Look up! Display plants on shelves, hang
them on the walls, suspend them from a
balcony railing, place them anywhere but
the floor.

Instagram

@jardinieresauvage

Growing up on a farm in Australia, plants and gardening were a constant in Rebecca's life. Her childhood was attuned to the seasons: from sun ripening the berries to mushrooms that popped up after rain. Gardening is in her heart.

A career in international diplomacy brought her to Paris, but when she was ready for a new challenge she opened Jardinière Sauvage. "I also love lamps and chairs, which would be more profitable than selling plants, but I wanted to share my love of gardening and sell something more than just a product. Plants are not things—they are life!"

Whether their goal is to plant seeds (local to the region) and keep their initial plant care quick and easy—or to really dig and get their hands dirty growing their own vegetables (even in the middle of the city) and saving seeds for the next season—all of Rebecca's customers want to learn and grow. "Gardening is like meditation; time to be in the present. Keeping a vegetable garden is hard work and heavy meditation, but I love and need it."

Even though Rebecca's apartment is a green oasis, with lush balconies on all sides, her eyes light up when she speaks of outdoor plants. "You can touch them, they react, you see them grow, and they give you produce or flowers. And through my Japanese pruning shears I communicate with them."

The plants and collections in Rebecca's Parisian apartment—from designer furniture to souvenirs to quirky finds and vintage treasures—make for an interesting mix. "I have a connection with all things I own; that's why I'm a hoarder. For example, the cowhides from Argentina that I brought back to Paris in my backpack have been with me for many, many years."

Rebecca also shares her passion and knowledge of greenery with her son, Aleksi. From an early age he has helped with plant care around the house. "He always gives me drawings of plants and flowers, and in the shop he loves to help water. When we're in the garden, he is barefoot just like me, to be grounded."

opposite, top left: In her kitchen Rebecca grows a small forest of avocado plants, a small citrus tree, and a lot of fresh herbs in the jardinière on the French balcony.

opposite, top right: Rebecca, Aleksi, and Baby Sand the teddy bear.

opposite, bottom: Sweetly scented blooms just outside the window add another level of enjoyment to the bedroom.

below: A robust watering can, a jardinière, and some terra-cotta pots in Rebecca's winter garden.

plant tribe stories . . .
Tish Carlson

"Plants are awesome!"

Location

Albuquerque, New Mexico, USA

Profession

Photographer, shop owner at
No Longer Wander Shop

Zodiac

Leo

Lives with

Husband Matt, daughters Kelsey and
Audrey, son Grayson, dog Lemon

Apartment size

2,000 square feet / 185 square meters

Favorite plant

Monstera deliciosa

Plant decor idea

Don't be afraid to hang up a really big
plant: It makes a real statement and
creates a jungle effect.

Number of plants

87

Instagram

@nolongerwander @nolongerwandershop

In a city that is famous for its desert landscape lives a family with "a thing" for plants. Although the climate is arid, that didn't keep Tish and her family from turning their home into a lush and stylish jungle. Quite the contrary actually. After growing up with a mom who was a passionate gardener, Tish felt inspired to grow houseplants, even before the trend gained momentum a few years ago. At first she wasn't very successful, but she stayed with it. "I was fascinated by how plants make a home happier once you bring them in. And I was inspired to learn and grow with plants. I bought a lot of houseplants and then killed them all. Matt said that I couldn't buy any greenery anymore, but I continued and that's where my plant story actually kicked off."

Tish eventually learned to grow plants that were local to the Southwest, and her success became a business: Today, she is the proprietor of No Longer Wander, a plant and decor shop. At home and at work, there are always plenty of plants to care for. "You can literally find plants in the kitchen sink (waiting to soak up water) every single day. [And] in the shop we have a dedicated sink that is just for plant care."

Tish's love for plants is infectious, inspiring both her customers and her three kids. "The kids love plants and actually chose the plants for their rooms by themselves. They even asked for a plant shelfie for their birthdays!" The next green generation is on its way!

opposite, top: The earthy living room features a selection of cacti, succulents, and a tall fiddle fig.

opposite, bottom left: Tish and Matt enjoy a happy life with their family and plants.

opposite, bottom right: A big
Thaumatophyllum xanadu hanging in the living room corner.

top: Kelsey and Audrey cuddle with Lemon.

above: Grayson loves plants, too. He chooses plants for his room by himself.

Andy Barlow

"Thanks to plants, I discovered
a passionate plant community and
made many plant-loving friends."

Location

Portland, Oregon, USA

Profession

Interior designer

Zodiac

Taurus

Lives with

Cats Cavanaugh and Claude

Apartment size

650 square feet / 60 square meters

Favorite plant

Ficus elastica

Plant decor idea

Every home has an awkward corner that
is difficult to design around, but here
is an easy solution: Put a plant there
(chosen according to the light situation)
and the awkward corner comes instantly
to life!

Number of plants

Approximately 50

Instagram

@pizza_affairs

A healthy snake plant welcomes the guests in the hallway of this stylish Portland home. Trailing pothos plants embellish the bookshelves, a *Dracaena* sits in the corner, and a mature fiddle fig completes the green surroundings in the living room. Clearly, this is the home of a plant lover.

Andy confesses, "My love for plants evolved over time. When I got my first plant, I immediately noticed how much life it brought into my home—just a single plant! So I started buying more and I have been adding plants into my home ever since. I cannot imagine a home without plants anymore."

But plants are much more than interior decoration for this member of the Plant Tribe: "Once I got into plants, I realized there is a whole plant community. I met friends and like-minded people I would not have met before my passion for plants," he adds enthusiastically.

below: Andy mixes vintage items with contemporary pieces and plants, resulting in a special Portland style.

opposite: Andy is an interior designer with a special love for plants.

top: The huge *Ficus lyrata*, also known as fiddle fig, adds instant character to Andy's living room. Ever since he found the right spot for it, it thrives!

above: The bedroom features only a few plants, but a botanical pillow doubles the effect.

chapter 4

WELL-BEING WITH PLANTS

A serene plant oasis in the buzzing district of Pinheiros in São Paulo, Brazil.

As plant owners, we think mostly about how to keep our plants happy, by finding a watering routine and tending to them: fertilizing them, cleaning their leaves, and repotting them. Too often we forget that our plants return the good we do, in multiple ways. In fact, plants do much more for us than we do for them. To live with plants is to make a commitment to your own well-being. Whether we are conscious of it or not, plants lift our moods, help us unwind, feed our souls, and relax our bodies. In other words, a home filled with plants is a free spa for your body and soul, and your foundation for a good, healthy, and balanced life.

The mere presence of plants seems to exert a magic force over human beings—plants engage our minds, refresh our bodies and spirits; they position us firmly in the moment.

Our profound connection to nature is captured in the term "biophilia," which is derived from the Greek words for "life" and "love." It describes our love for nature and all living things. Oliver Sacks writes that "nature calls to something very deep in us," and that biophilia is "an essential part of the human condition." The restorative powers of plants have been known from the earliest days of humanity. So it's only logical that in a modern home, too, plants will boost our well-being.

plant ideas for your mind, body, and soul

Take a moment out of your day just for you. Spend two minutes brushing your teeth while watching your plants, or relax in the presence of your houseplants.

Replenishing our minds, bodies, and souls can be simple. All we need to do is allow ourselves the time to unwind from the daily grind of our lives. And surround ourselves with plants of course. Here are a few ideas to help you improve your well-being.

TAKE A PLANT BATH

The practice of *shinrin-yoku* (forest bathing) was developed in Japan in the 1980s, and is today a cornerstone of preventive health care and healing in Japanese medicine. What works in a forest also works in your urban jungle at home.

To experience the soothing and balancing power of a plant bath, simply surround yourself with all your plants—the more the merrier. Find a moment when you're grouping your plants together for plant care, or just take a seat (or, even better, lie down on a blanket or floor cushion) in the greenest corner of your home. Try to be fully encircled by plants—ideally, when you look up you'll see some foliage, too. And now it's really up to you! Do whatever relaxes you. You can simply sit in the midst of your plants, or read a book or a magazine, or sip a cup of coffee or tea. Give yourself fifteen minutes or even half an hour. Clear your mind of the daily buzz, switch your phone off, and focus on yourself and your inner balance. The plants will help you relax. Give it a try and trust your feelings. If you choose to sit quietly among your plants, see if you can focus on your breathing. Breathe steadily and calmly, and take deep breaths—inhale through your nose, exhale through your mouth. Fill your body with oxygen. The plants around you are producing fresh oxygen to restore your body and mind. Open up all your senses; tune in and experience every minute consciously. You'll feel relaxed and balanced afterward. You're then good to go and resume your busy schedule!

START A PLANT PROJECT

In addition to biophilia, Oliver Sacks writes about the human desire to tend and manage nature, which he calls "hortophilia." Now, if you're lucky enough to have a garden, go outside and practice hortophilia. Start a gardening project. Or if you have a balcony, how about beginning to grow some vegetables on it? If you have neither, start a windowsill plant project at home.

Why? Because tending to plants is utterly relaxing and comforting. It's not a chore; consider it self-care and creative time for your imagination. A plant project helps take your mind off to-do lists, setbacks, and emotional roller coasters—trust us and give it a try. Your plants will be your best partners and friends, helping you clear your mind and getting you back on track. Simple plant projects you can make at home include building a terrarium, growing plants from seed, and growing new plants from cuttings. Use your imagination and do what makes you happy!

Creating a simple terrarium in a glass vessel can be both calming and rewarding. Here a little *Begonia rex* sits in a glass jar.

MEDITATE WITH PLANTS

Spending time with plants can have the same effect on our minds as meditation. So including a meditation practice among plants in your weekly routine will double the benefit. Here are a few ideas about how to meditate, and raise your level of mindfulness, in the company of your plants:

Breathing meditation

Sit surrounded by plants—in your home, garden, or balcony. Make yourself comfortable and look at your plants. Breathe naturally and take in the beauty of nature around you. If you wish, set a mantra for your meditation. Use a positive formulation, like "I am peaceful," "I am loving," "I am grateful," and so on. Now close your eyes and focus on your breathing. Take a deep, full breath, inhaling through your nose; fill your stomach with oxygen first, and then your chest. Now exhale through your mouth, releasing the air from your stomach first, and then from your chest. Continue breathing in this way for a few minutes, until your body is fully revitalized with fresh oxygen (your plants will be producing that oxygen, by the way). Now return to breathing normally and let go of any thoughts. Be in the moment, feel your body, and be grateful for all the good things in your life.

Listening meditation

Take a seat among your plants, as in the breathing meditation. Keep your eyes open, however, and contemplate the shapes of the plants' leaves and the tiniest details of their patterns and perforations; observe the plants' stems, branches, and soil. As you do so, clear your mind of everyday chatter. Be mindful and present in the moment. You'll feel invigorated after ten to fifteen minutes in silence with your plants. You'll also be in good shape to start a round of plant care after your meditation.

Sketchbook meditation

This variation is especially for those of you who love to use your imaginations and who find inner peace and balance through activity. Follow the steps for the listening meditation, but now go one step further! Put your observations into words or sketches! Use a small sketchbook and get creative—write what you see, what you feel. Or draw the plants, the leaves, or whatever comes from your inner being. Let go of constraints and don't judge whether the words make sense, or whether the sketch looks good. Just follow your inner voice and your intuition. Your writing or drawing is not the ultimate goal—what you seek is inner peace and balance. But, hey, if the end result is a nice plant poem or a quirky plant sketch—frame it and remind yourself that you're always at peace among your plants!

Walk in nature

- Spending time in nature has long been considered beneficial to our overall well-being. Nature triggers a meditative state of mind and a greater sense of happiness. Imagine a sunny spring day in a forest or meadow and the array of flowers, colors, shades of green—who wouldn't be caught smiling? Nature works its magic! But how is that? Nature has a way of demanding our full attention. It forces us to focus and look at what lies before us. In other words, when we're in nature we become present. Allow time to take in the lush natural world around you; if you don't have your own garden, head to your local botanical garden or a park. Awaken your senses by seeing, smelling, hearing, and feeling what is around you. Be mindful when walking in nature and come back home rested, balanced, and calmed—and at the same time invigorated.

- A recent study by Aarhus University, in Denmark, found that growing up in green surroundings lowers the risk of developing various mental disorders later in life by 55 percent. For more on Aarhus University, see https://international.au.dk/

above: Surround yourself with personal items that have meaning to you. These will always enhance your inner balance and happiness.

right: Renato (see page 152) preparing a clay mask for a time-out moment in the plant-filled bathroom.

above: Ferns, pothos, and philodendrons are great choices for high-humidity areas such as bathrooms.

right: Lucas (see page 152) and his plants enjoying a "plant bath." He keeps humidity-loving plants such as *Tillandsia*, bromeliads, and philodendrons around the bathtub. This way they both enjoy a moment of well-being.

opposite: Mounted staghorn ferns above the tub are not only decorative but practical, too. The steam keeps the ferns humid and thriving.

ESTABLISH YOUR OWN PLANT RITUAL

There are all sorts of possibilities for plant rituals in your daily life, whether at home or outdoors (see chapter 1). Here's a suggestion for your weekly routine: Create a green spa, for your ultimate time-out. We all know that a hot bath can work wonders after a stressful day. If you combine this with the power of plants, you'll lift your spirits to unknown spheres. How? Simple as this: Even if your bathroom has no sunlight and you have no plants there, group a few leafy plants near the tub and then draw a bath. Tropicals, which love a high level of humidity, are best.

Add anything to your tub that makes you happy and relaxed—essential oils or dried flowers and plants. How about sage or mint leaves or rosemary sprigs from your balcony or kitchen? Add dried rose petals, orange blossoms, or marigolds. Do whatever pleases your senses. Also add a crystal or two—a rose quartz, amethyst, or apatite is ideal. Light a scented candle, if you like, have a glass of red wine or tea, and let your mind float and your senses unwind. Now enjoy your green spa, surrounded by plants—and you and they will benefit equally. The plants will calm you down and bring the soothing vibe of nature to your bathroom, and simultaneously enjoy the high humidity and warm temperature themselves. A win-win, and truly one of our favorite plant rituals at home.

well-being with plants

141

slow living with plants

Plants have the ability to ground us and take the speed and buzz out of our daily lives.

Nature in general and plants in particular are the best teachers of a slow, mindful way of living. Plants take time to grow; they're not in a rush. They take time to develop strong roots and new leaves and stems; they bloom only when the season is right and the conditions are favorable. For us, appreciating this slowness is a first step toward embracing a slower-paced lifestyle. From plants we learn to be patient and to take one step after the other. Growing and thriving take time—for both plants and human beings. Today we need to remind ourselves more than ever of the importance of taking our time.

For your personal well-being, stay aware of social pressure and the feeling that you must accept every invitation to go out. Enjoy life with your loved ones and grant yourself those moments of joy and happiness at home.

"I'm busy!" When a friend asks us to meet for coffee, we have to check our schedules. Our phones are buzzing. And when they're not, we're catching up on the latest episodes of our favorite TV series while looking out for spoilers on social media. In other words, we're constantly busy.

In these overconnected times, being busy and on top of it all is presented as the norm. We're supposed to have picture-perfect lives (and picture-perfect plants, for that matter). And when we don't, and we're spending a Friday night on the couch scrolling through social media updates and seeing that everyone else is hanging out at a festival or tending to their thriving plants, we feel bad. It's impossible for us not to want to be at whatever place some incredible thing is happening because we suffer from FOMO, the fear of missing out. And this fear is a serious threat to our well-being. Envy is the art of counting someone else's blessings, instead of our own. And we don't want that!

Choose to spend time by yourself, and create deeper relationships with your family members and friends, without the interruption of buzzing phones. Take things slowly and focus on what's important in life. Since you're a member of the Plant Tribe, one way you can spend time by yourself is in tending to your plants. How can plants help you with your slow living? Here are a few ideas:

well-being with plants

Sometimes you simply feel joy when staying in—just like Toy (see page 32). A cup of coffee, a good book, and the company of your plants can be just a perfect alternative to any social event.

Care for your plants

Make your plant care routine a conscious exercise of patience. Don't rush. Instead, carve out some extra time for you and your plants. Make it a weekly #MeMoment, with an hour dedicated to your well-being and that of your plants. Such a routine should leave both you and your plants happy, balanced, and relaxed.

Keep a plant journal

Writing in a plant journal can be beneficial in two ways: First, it assists you with your plant care and is a record of your plant growing process. Second, it helps you slow down. Take your time recording the names of your plants, their watering preferences, what soil they like, and the light conditions that are ideal for them. Note your successes as well as your failures in caring for them. By keeping a plant journal, you'll not only learn more about your plants; you'll also learn to consciously take your time.

Grow edibles

Whether it's on your kitchen windowsill, on your balcony, or in a small garden, growing edibles is a deeply centering and rewarding exercise in slow living. Sowing seeds or seedlings, caring for them regularly, and finally harvesting the fruits of your labor is a long process, and cannot be rushed. Knowing how much time and effort went into growing the food on your plate will give you a profound appreciation of nature's cycles. This resonates with our understanding of a good and meaningful life. The final result is not only a delicious homegrown meal but also the nourishing feeling of contentment. In other words, you are growing food for your body and for your soul.

Give yourself permission to live in the present. Be easy on yourself and treat yourself to a relaxing evening when you've had a bad day—or even when you've received good news: Take a moment to embrace it and celebrate accordingly. Enjoy social media–free time and unfollow people who trigger your FOMO or bring negativity into your life. Practice saying no.

Experiencing true happiness and treasuring every moment are what it's all about. Prioritize your time and cherish JOMO, the joy of missing out.

horticultural therapy

Dried herbs and flowers not only look decorative; some also have
therapeutic properties and can serve as remedies for your own well-being.

As members of the Plant Tribe, we know subconciously that caring for plants helps us to be fully in the present. Even young children can benefit from mindfulness or meditation workshops in school, as their active lives, with a large variety of extracurricular activities and increased pressure to perform in a competitive environment, diminish their time and ability to just be kids. These workshops teach them to trust their instincts and to listen to their feelings, and give them time and quiet in which to gain self-confidence. Small plant projects, either in school or at home, can build on that foundation. Some of us may remember growing sunflowers, alfalfa sprouts, or papyrus plants in school—small biology experiments featuring foolproof and rapidly developing greenery that taught us the proper way to tend to plants. While some of us were hooked on growing greenery from early childhood, the majority of us lost touch with it. What a joy to (re)discover it as young-at-heart adults!

We referenced Oliver Sacks at the beginning of this chapter on the importance of gardens. This is especially the case when we're going through a tough time, whether we're suffering from a serious physical or mental health problem or "just" a heartbreak. Tending to plants is so powerful that it can be used in the process of healing.

Horticultural therapy combines the art and science of growing flowers, vegetables, fruits, and trees with the most current theories of human behavior, neuroscience, and psychotherapy. Through gardening activities, horticultural therapists seek to enhance patients' social, cognitive, and physiological functioning, with the primary goal of improving health and inspiring motivation for change. By placing patients in caregiving roles—for example, by having them plant vegetables in a garden or propagate plants from a hospital bed—the therapists are able to create experiential environments that are both growth-focused and life-affirming.

HEALTH BENEFITS OF TENDING TO PLANTS

Horticultural therapy can help in the treatment of many health issues, such as:

- PTSD
- Eating disorders
- Physical rehabilitation
- Improvement of fine motor skills
- Pain
- Memory improvement
- Task initiation
- Language skills
- Socialization

In a hospital, where everything is stressful and attention is often focused on the physical health of the patient, tending to a plant allows a complete change of perspective. The patient is no longer the object—the plant is—and this gives the patient space to heal and focus on aspects of the recovery process that doctors may overlook. Bringing nontoxic plants and soil into a sterile hospital environment can be tricky, but the sanitary risks are minimal when there are clearly established procedures for staff and patients.

Take care of your own well-being and health; look to nature for inspiration and for the knowledge that a good and healthy life is not one of rushing and grabbing all opportunities. It's one that is based on growing steadily and quietly, with patience and contentment. It's one nourished by the simplest ingredients: love, light, and natural food. Stay healthy, stay happy, and take care of your plants! They'll reward you many times over!

plant tribe stories . . .

Olive May

"Plants transformed my life;
they opened so many doors for me!"

Location

Dallas, Texas, USA

Profession

Teacher, educational consultant

Zodiac

Virgo

Lives with

Husband Rudy and dogs Mylee and Fender

House size

3,000 square feet / 278 square meters

Favorite plant

Ficus benjamina

Plant decor idea

Add character and fun to your plants with artsy-looking head-shaped planters, or planters with faces.

Number of plants

350

Instagram

@oliveinwanderland

A spacious house in a peaceful residential area of Dallas is home to Olive and Rudy, a teacher couple who have been together since their teens. These high school sweethearts love to work on their home, and they have renovated steadily to transform it into an artistic haven. Houseplants can be found in every corner, and now—more than 350 plants later—they are still making space for a few more. "Estate sales are a great way to find mature plants for a reasonable price. Or check local nurseries and Facebook Marketplace in your region for good plant deals," Olive advises.

Olive's love for plants is inherited from her mom, who owns an even bigger collection. At one point, when their communication was strained, Olive would reach out to her mom for plant advice. This strengthened their relationship, and their bond grew with each plant Olive added to her collection. Today, her mom happily acts as plant sitter whenever the couple is away. "Caring for plants has been a revelation: They have helped me overcome anxiety and have taught me to be more patient. I don't worry so much about myself when I care for plants. They have helped me heal, for which I'm very thankful."

Plants have also led Olive to the discovery of new creative outlets, like painting and pottery. Olive wanted unique planters for her green friends and began making lighthearted head-shaped planters that are now displayed all over the house. "Recently I visited a succulent grower in Austin and they asked if I could make some head planters for their shop, too! The love for plants has connected me to amazing like-minded people."

Saturday mornings are reserved for a weekly plant check—and the cactus room gets special attention on the first and fifteenth of the month, when its inhabitants are watered. "I once bought a beautiful old cactus from a guy who wanted four hundred dollars for it but eventually sold it to me for much less because he wanted the plant to be in good hands and keep thriving. Plants are worth more than money."

And we can only agree.

opposite, top left: Olive and Rudy live a happy life and are proud Texans.

opposite, top right: Olive's beauty corner in her bedroom is lush and green with snake plants and a tall *Ficus alii*.

opposite, below right: Use similar planters, like this collection of "face pots," to create a striking vignette.

opposite, bottom: Olive's sunroom is filled with cacti and succulents enjoying all-day sunshine.

below: Olive is a creative soul and derives lots of inspiration from her plants.

plant tribe stories . . .
Lucas Midio

"There are no ugly plants—people just don't know enough about them."

Location

São Paulo, Brazil

Profession

Freelance game artist, plant consultant

Zodiac

Gemini

Lives with

Partner Renato and dog Nuno

Apartment size

1,290 square feet / 120 square meters

Favorite plant

Vriesea saundersii

Plant decor idea

Use branches and natural materials to hang plants. Group plants according to their natural habitat (mountain, desert, jungle) or by shape (rosettes, spiky plants, and so on).

Number of plants

Approximately 100

Instagram

@mi.di.o @renato.apf

opposite, top: View out of Lucas
and Renato's apartment at the
Santa Cecília church in the
namesake São Paulo neighborhood.

opposite, bottom left: Lucas and
Renato love plants, midcentury
design, vintage finds, and
indigenous craftsmanship from
Brazil. But above all, they love
their dog, Nuno.

opposite, bottom right: A vintage
tapestry sets the tone in the
warm, ochre-colored bedroom.

above: Lucas has a talent for
creating plant stylings with
vintage ceramics and tribal art,
while Renato is a passionate
vinyl collector.

São Paulo's buzzing Santa Cecília neighborhood is home to cool bars, delicious restaurants, Friday-night samba performances on the street, and the beautiful urban jungle of Lucas and Renato and their dog, Nuno. Their spacious flat overlooks Santa Cecília's central square and charms visitors with worn and beautiful details: old tiles in the bathroom and on the balcony, a lived-in and beautiful wooden floor, carefully curated midcentury furniture, and an earthy color palette. Throughout the warm and inviting home are rich details such as Brazilian folk-art objects, woven baskets from Amazonas, jugs from Minas Gerais, and wooden figurines made by indigenous tribes. Of course, another thing that captures attention is the abundance of plants—most of them native to Brazil, a particular passion for Lucas.

"Whenever I head out to buy one plant, I come back with at least three," says Lucas with a smile. At the beginning of their life together, Renato was less at ease with the abundance of plants. "At the beginning, the plants seemed like objects that often were in the way," confesses Renato. Today, both Renato and Lucas agree on how much the plants contribute to their well-being, and their sense of home.

Lucas's love for plants began during his childhood in the countryside of Brazil. He fondly remembers joyful days in the Atlantic Forest, playing among bromeliads, philodendrons, orchids, epiphytes, ferns, and other tropical plants. A lot of plant knowledge was passed to him by his grandmother, who was a real expert of the local flora. Lucas recalls, "When I was a teenager, I wanted to escape all that and be a big city boy. It wasn't until I came to São Paulo that I felt something was missing in my life. Adding plants to my home was a way to reconnect to my family and my roots."

chapter 5

GET CREATIVE WITH PLANTS

Artists and other creative people have flourished among plants for centuries—they drew, they wrote, they composed. Plants have always touched the human soul in the best way possible. Nature— the beauty of lush foliage, the ever-changing colors and shapes, the timelessness, the birth and rebirth—inherently ignites inspiration; nature's poetic dimensions are many and magnificent. But there is even a scientific way to account for plants' impact on creativity.

Did you know that the human eye is better at perceiving green than any other color in the universe? Humans are trichromats, which means that we perceive three primary colors: blue, green, and red. The retinas in our eyes can detect light between wavelengths of 400 and 700 nanometers (nm), from blue at 400 nm to green at around 550 nm, to yellow, orange, and red at 700 nm. Green being located in the middle of the visible spectrum, some scientists believe that because our eyes are at the peak of their perception to detect the wavelengths that correspond with the color green, the hue calms us down. Our nervous system can relax when looking at green; the color is one of balance and harmony. On a primitive level we are reassured by green because it indicates the presence of water and thus less danger of famine. Reassurance is also what we feel when we enter a lush botanical garden, walk through a leafy green forest, take a so-called plant bath, or simply visit a local garden center: It is refreshing and calming, and we are aware of the present. Being out in nature also quiets a part of the brain called the subgenual prefrontal cortex, decreasing our tendency to dwell on problems, making us feel more carefree and relaxed. No wonder why we, as a Plant Tribe, are compelled to add these qualities to our own homes and work spaces!

above: A creative corner in the
room of Júlia Anadam (see page
58) with collected items. Books,
stones, patterns, and colors as
well as scents provide a wealth of
inspiration to kick-start creative
projects.

opposite: To boost your creativity,
spend time in nature, observing and
collecting. Nature has inspired
humankind since ancient times.
Gather little collections of rare
stones, crystals, pine cones,
shells, and other natural objects
to display in your home.

creativity at work

Tribal ceramics brought back from a trip to Colombia sit playfully on Alina's mantel.

We believe that adding plants to your work environment is a must: Caring for an office plant, or an entire jungle, creates an opportunity to have a little break from work, dig in the soil, prune, water, and just be present with the plant while forgetting about the stressful meeting you just had or that upcoming deadline. Did you know that a few plants in the office can reduce blood pressure and even prompt more generous behavior toward others? Plants are also great conversation starters: Give them name tags so that your colleagues can ask how you and "George" are doing today. And while you're on vacation, ask your colleagues to help keep "George" alive. If you don't want your colleagues to worry about your plants, use a watering globe or terra-cotta watering cone during your absence.

Working surrounded by plants gives you an instant boost of energy and helps you focus on daily tasks—or provides some distraction. The presence of houseplants on your desk refreshes your ability to concentrate because it is passive but also stimulating. It allows your eyes to wander during the day, to appreciate the irregular shapes of a leaf, the interesting patterns, the deep green color . . . When we visited Alina Fassakhova in New York City (see page 194), she told us that the presence of plants help her rest her eyes after intense hours of concentration painting a new canvas. It's essential to her work as an artist to look at greenery and to touch and smell the leaves.

(see page 194)

above: Alina finds inspiration and serenity in her plants while painting in her Manhattan home. The shapes and colors inspire her organic paintings, while the sight of plants also soothes her eyes after long painting sessions.

right: Alina's painting overflows with colors and organic lines. This one is reminiscent of a flower.

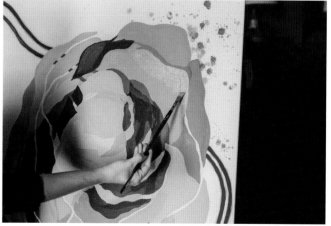

when plants drive a business

The green home office of Toy Taniel in São Paulo, Brazil.

The organic shapes of plants and the abundance of textures invite us to explore our own creativity, whether in our daily work, in our relationships with others, or by actually making something by hand. Nature, and plants in particular, offers endless inspiration. Plants spark so much joy in some people that they launch an entire business around them. We spoke with three creatives who turned their passion for plants and design into thriving companies.

Designer Tim Labenda (see page 202) creating in his Berlin home office, which features a big *Monstera deliciosa*.

Samantha Leung

Location

Seattle, Washington, USA

Company

HEMLEVA: enameled pins and key chains, air plants, hanging Himmeli ornaments, and more

Favorite plant

Sansevieria

Instagram

@hemleva

What made you start HEMLEVA?

HEMLEVA began in a pretty nontraditional way. I was in intense physical therapy for a while, and I needed to occupy my time. I started HEMLEVA with one hundred dollars and told myself that whether I make it or I don't, at least I'll know that I tried my hardest. To this day I still hand make each and every hanging ornament to order.

When did plants enter your life?

One of my earliest memories is of visiting the botanical gardens with my mom and grandmother. We would slowly walk through each of the different greenhouses and gardens, breathing in the dense humidity and the smell of fresh earth. Plants remind me of a simpler time, spent with people I love.

Has your relationship with plants changed now that you're working with plants?

I love plants even more now than when I started my business. I have met so many fellow plant aficionados and collectors—and something they all have in common is they are so kind, supportive, and giving.

Tell us about your customers.

There have been so many instances where people tell me that one of my products reminds them of someone they love or someone they lost touch with, and that's something that I never expected when I started this business—to make something that went beyond being pretty, or functional, and is also meaningful.

What part do plants have in your home life and your work life?

I firmly believe that you should fill your space with things that bring you joy, and for me that means that there are houseplants and lots of *Tillandsia*. I can't help but think of them whenever I water or tend to the plants. Instead of scent memories, for me there are plant memories.

What role does sustainability play in your work?

For my Himmeli and wall sconces, I purchase raw materials from the United States, to decrease my carbon footprint; I offer plastic-free packaging for my key chains, and I am moving toward completely plastic-free shipping materials.

What is your dream project for HEMLEVA?

To design plant propagation accessories: It would mean so much to make it easier to grow, care for, and share plants.

Fanny Zedenius

Location

Stockholm, Sweden

Company

Createaholic: handmade macramé
decor and DIY supplies

Favorite plant

Rubber plant

Instagram

@createaholic

What made you start Createaholic?

I discovered macramé when I was searching
for ways to fit more plants in my home.
Soon afterward I started mass-producing
macramé plant hangers and decided
to launch a business! Plants were an
important part of my brand from the get-go.

Have you always worked as a creative?

No, I studied international relations and
worked for the Swedish National Committee
for UN Women for a while. I always
thought that my hobby had to remain just
that, a hobby.

When did plants enter your life?

I distinctly remember my first plant,
which I got when I was about six,
was from a cutting of a *Peperomia
obtusifolia*. I watched it grow roots in
the water and then planted it and watched
it grow, and I became the plant lover I
am today! My mother told me that plants
like it when we talk to them and tell
them nice things, so I talked to that
plant a lot.

Do you have a plant ritual?

I sit with my fiddle-leaf fig tree for
a couple of minutes every day and shake
it a bit to simulate a tropical storm. I
heard this could help fiddle figs grow a
thicker trunk. It's a commitment because
the trunk won't adjust straightaway, but
I'm in it for the long haul!

What part do plants have in your home life and your work life?

I work from home, so plants are a
constant feature in both private and work
life. Our apartment has large windows,
with plants as privacy screens, but
the main reason for having so many is
simply that I love them. I honestly can't
imagine not having plants around me; they
have such a calming and uplifting effect.
Simon [my husband] and I joke that they
are our babies.

Do you celebrate business successes in a special way? For example, by adopting a new plant?

Treating myself to a new plant is my
favorite way of celebrating.

What role does sustainability play in your work?

Sustainability is something I prioritize.
This includes evaluating my use of
plastics, asking suppliers to avoid
plastic packing, searching for organic
materials, and lots more.

What's your dream project for Createaholic?

Having a collection of more high-end wall
hangings and a gallery exhibition.

get creative with plants

Octávio Meireles

Location

Brasília, Brazil

Company

Plantestilo: plants and landscaping

Favorite plant

String of hearts

Instagram

@plantestilo

What made you start Plantestilo?

I majored in international relations and intended to follow a completely different path, but when I was studying for my public service exams, I got very stressed. The one thing that eased my mind was my garden and work with plants. Before I knew it, I was creating my very own fertilizer, then vases, and then my own arrangements. For the first time in my life, I felt absolutely whole. In short, I launched my business to explore the utter joy plants brought to me.

When did plants enter your life?

Growing up, I used to sneak into my maternal grandma's garage and chew on the stems of her begonia (they are edible and have a distinctive sour flavor). And also, I loved the way my paternal grandma used to tell me stories about the plants and their names.

Has your relationship with plants changed now that you're working with plants?

I love what I do, and I cannot look at a room without thinking of a thousand different projects for it.

Tell us about your customers.

The question they ask most is, Which plant can you get me that I will be least likely to kill?! People nowadays live such hectic lives and are always trying to combine style with manageability.

Do you have a plant ritual?

The first thing I do when I walk into my store is to take a deep breath and let my gratitude that I am able to do this work for another day sink in. I then check on each plant individually and make a mental list of everything I need to get done that day.

Do you celebrate business successes in a special way? For example, by adopting a new plant?

I celebrate successes with everyone who helped me get to where I am. Plants feed off energy, and I think they take some of my positive energy with them when they go to new homes.

What role does sustainability play in your work?

We work with a plant's natural life cycle and without artificial greenhouses. Every leaf that drops is put into our compost, as part of our zero-waste policy. Our fertilizer is 100 percent organic matter.

What is your dream project for Plantestilo?

For every plant I sell and for every vertical garden I create to send a little piece of me with them.

Viktoria Dahlberg's stock of
N5 & SUNNY designs in her
green home office.

dress your plants

A branch or driftwood can be easily transformed into an unexpected plant holder. Here, Lucas used a branch to hang some of his air plants.

Think of your collection of plants: Whether you have two plants, twenty plants, or two hundred, they most likely have different shapes, colors, structures, and sizes. But what about their pots? Are they potted in terra-cotta pots, vintage earthenware, synthetic pots, glass containers, fiberglass planters, or contemporary ceramics? Or have you kept them in their plastic nursery or grow pots?

Dressing your plants, by choosing the style of pots for your home, is a personal affair. Some of us prefer plain terra-cotta pots; their natural brown-orange color makes the foliage pop, their weight makes them a steady base for plants, and they are some of the most affordable pots on the market. And because they have been around for decades, you can find the prettiest vintage ones, with mineral deposits on the inside and outside that give them that extra charm. Even if you prefer keeping your palette very terra-cotta but like a more contemporary aesthetic, you can find exceptional pots in terra-cotta that truly stand out, as the material has inspired many designers to get creative. In Olive and Rudy's home (see page 148) in Dallas, you'll find mostly terra-cotta pots, but some of them have faces: Olive and Rudy added an unexpected twist to the uniform palette of their pots. Our Spanish friends at livingthings created Voltasol, a rolling flowerpot that can turn because of its semi-conical base. Design brands like Ferm Living, Nick Fraser, Skagerak, and Umbra

Shift also have very contemporary takes on the terra-cotta pot in their collections.

Terra-cotta literally means "baked earth" and is a clay-like earthenware ceramic that can be either glazed or unglazed. When it's unglazed, the material is very porous, so the soil dries out faster, letting the roots and potting mix breathe. This means terra-cotta is slightly more suited to plants that thrive in drier soil than to tropical foliage. But if you have a better understanding of the needs of your planty tropical friends, you can let them thrive in terra-cotta pots. Or apply a nontoxic cement sealer, which is made for porous materials, to your pots. You can also use spray paint to seal your pots, but you may want to avoid that with your herbs and edible plants.

If you think that terra-cotta pots are boring: Did you know that terra-cotta (the material) doesn't just come in "terra-cotta"? Since earth, the main element of terra-cotta pots, doesn't have the same color and composition everywhere in the world, terra-cotta pots can be different colors. The traditional Iranian pots available from KHASHKHASH are proof: Their colors vary from yellow to blush to beige to deep orange and red.

opposite, top left: This cute legged terra-cotta "Tri-Pot" by Studio Arhoj adds height to a glacier pothos.

opposite, top right: This geometric white planter, which holds a *Peperomia*, recalls the shape of an ancient vessel.

opposite, bottom left: Set plant cuttings in decorative glass vases for a modern, clean look.

opposite, bottom right: Baskets are perfect plant containers: They add texture and style, and you can hide an unspectacular plant pot inside or keep your plant in the nursery plant pot with a little saucer underneath.

below: Cacti, moss, and stones are decoratively arranged in a flat, white bowl. Make sure to use a layer of pebbles or sand for drainage in pots without drainage holes.

pot materials

Playing with materials and textures is common when styling interiors.
The same is valid when choosing plant pots made of different materials.

SYNTHETIC POTS

Made from non-recycled or recycled plastic, they keep moisture inside the pot and are lightweight, which is ideal when you like to move your plants around a lot.

VINTAGE STONEWARE OR EARTHENWARE POTS

These are fired at a high temperature, which reduces the pots' porousness and vulnerability to the elements. If a ceramic pot is left out in the cold weather, however, it can crack.

GLASS CONTAINERS

These allow you to see some of the roots through the glass, which is always interesting, but the algae and moisture in the soil, and the lack of drainage holes, can cause the glass to become greenish and the plant to feel poorly because of moist roots. Glass jars, bottles, lab flasks, and test tubes come in handy, however, when you want to propagate cuttings.

CONTEMPORARY CERAMIC POTS

The designs are endless, but the majority of these ceramics come without drainage holes and are to be used as cachepots—to cover the grow pot. There is nothing that a good drill can't fix, however: Delicately drill one or more holes in the bottom of the pot so that excess water can leave the pot. Or if you are a trained plant parent: Cover the bottom of the pot with clay balls or terra-cotta shards, use water sparingly, and make sure water doesn't stagnate around the roots and cause root rot.

FIBERGLASS POTS

The lightweight material allows the creation of oversize pots that have the same moisture-retaining characteristics as synthetic pots. Some have the look of concrete.

BASKETS

The secret to a bohemian look with large plants in beautiful handcrafted baskets is to not pot the plants directly in the basket. Simply place the plant in its pot on a saucer inside the basket and remove the plant to water.

RESIN POTS

These are lightweight and come in a wide variety of shapes. Some, like the handmade pots from Capra Designs, even have matching saucers.

METAL PLANTERS

The biggest issue with metal planters is not the (possible) rust (iron oxide is insoluble in water and doesn't get to the roots) but that metal pots are prone to overheating, and excessive heat in a container can stress, damage, or even cook plants' roots. Copper is toxic to air plants, and, as with brass and zinc versions, it's better to use copper planters as decorative cachepots that conceal the grow pots. Powder-coated metal is safer for plants, as long as you keep the planter from becoming a stove for your plants.

TIN CANS

To prevent nicely decorated or plain tin cans from rusting when you use them as planters, coat the inside twice with clear enamel rust-resistant spray paint. Make sure to cover the creases, seams, and rims. Don't place the cans on a sunny windowsill, because the sun will cook the plants' roots.

CONCRETE POTS

High-quality concrete pots are 100 percent waterproof, and if they don't have drainage holes, you can use them as you would contemporary ceramic pots.

CACHEPOTS

The easiest way to instantly update a pot is by inserting it into a nicely decorated cachepot. These come in stiff neoprene (at Pijama) or slouchy cotton (at Skinny laMinx), or you can make one yourself (see page 181).

FELT POTS

Made from hand-felted wool, these pots give your plants a warm, cozy feeling, as if from a snug winter sweater. Those from Aveva Design are sealed on the inside with natural rubber, so you can water your plants without destroying the felt.

opposite, top left: Group planters of the same material together. This is a simple way to make a plant grouping visually coherent and appealing.

opposite, right: Use plant stands to play with height—you can place terra-cotta pots on metal plant stands and add an unusual basket for a visual surprise.

opposite, bottom left: Glass vessels, bowls, mugs, and a light bulb—get creative when choosing the materials for your plant pots.

below: Always a good idea for plant lovers—keep extra terra-cotta pots on hand for new plants that you acquire over time.

creative projects

Plant shelves become more interesting when they hold a mix of objects:
Here, handmade ceramics, crystals, candles, and found objects mingle with
a few plants on vintage shelves.

Being surrounded by plants can fuel a creative project that has nothing
to do with greenery. But it is equally fun to be creative with your plants
by updating the look of their planters or making them a new home in
the form of a hand-knotted plant hanger or plant stand. Here's a list,
by no means exhaustive, of easy creative projects for you . . . and your
houseplants:

Alina creates a green
wall with her pothos by
using simple, invisible
cable hooks. The effect
is stunning; an easy DIY
idea for every home!

Simple, stylish, and practical: Jennifer makes clever terrarium lamps by filling a large glass jar with terrarium potting mix and plants such as *Fittonia*, *Peperomia*, or little ferns. She finishes the project by adding a lamp socket and lampshade.

- PAINT OLD CERAMIC POTS with chalk paint to give them a new look. You don't even need to prime or seal the paint, as chalk paint can be applied to any porous surface.

- MAKE YOUR OWN CACHEPOT from left-over fabric or old cushion covers and curtains. You don't need a sewing machine or professional sewing skills for this: Fold a rectangular piece of fabric in two, with the right side on the inside. With some simple stitches sew the longer sides and one shorter side together. Turn the tube right side out. Place a tray in the base of the tube to keep the cachepot from becoming wet and stained. Insert the pot into the cachepot and fold over the unfinished top until it just covers the pot inside.

- GO THRIFT SHOPPING: You'll find the best treasures at garage sales, thrift shops, and secondhand markets. Remember: If the color of the pot is not your style, paint it to match your color scheme. Focus on the shape and size of the pot. Check out vases, too, as some tall vases have enough space for plants and their roots. Small glassware items can be used as a propagation station (see page 104), and basically any container, like a fruit bowl, a trash can, a boot, a kids' toy, or a baby bathtub, can be turned into a pot.

- THRIFTED CAKE STANDS, pie trays, oven dishes, and pudding bowls are stylish alternatives to cheap plastic plant trays. Or spray-paint faceted glass bowls and use them as saucers.

- STACK POTS OF DIFFERENT SIZES and shapes and glue them together to create a plant totem pole.

- JOIN A POTTERY CLASS and create your own pots and saucers.

- KNOT YOUR OWN PLANT HANGER from ribbons, fabric, yarn, or cotton cord.

- CREATE A PLANT STAND from wooden broomsticks and copper connectors, or use the frame of an old lampshade as a stand to hold a pot.

- DRY THE WILTED LEAVES of your plants in a flower press, or inside a heavy book weighted on top. When the leaves are fully dried you can frame them as souvenirs of the once happy leaves of your plant.

- ATTEND A TERRARIUM WORKSHOP and create your own miniature jungle.

- CREATE YOUR OWN PROPAGATION CONE from some water-resistant fabric. Cut out a circle with a 5-inch (13 cm) diameter and cut a hole in the middle with a diameter of 1 inch (2.5 cm). Remove one-eighth of the full circle and stitch the two ends together to create a cone. Use the propagation cone on top of a glass jar to grow an avocado seed (see page 101) or to keep a cutting from falling into the water.

simple plant styling tricks

Plant styling gets even more interesting when you add other decorative
elements into the mix. An unusual vase, fresh flowers, a personal collection—
the results look appealing and effortless.

When your plants are thriving and they are potted in pots that suit your interior decorating style, what else can you do to make them look their best and have the most visual impact in your home? Try any of these simple (but magic) tricks:

CREATE A "PLANT GANG"

The number-one advice for anyone who owns more than four houseplants is to gather them in a group. Think of them as you would when you take a family photo: The taller ones go in the back, the children in the front. Pair a spiky cactus with a leafy banana plant, a patterned *Calathea,* a bushy *Dracaena,* and a deep red *Oxalis triangularis* for an interesting mix. And remember *the* famous styling trick: Uneven numbers work best when displaying several items together.

For impact, group your plant gang in a single area and add unusual accents like the traditional ceramics from Colombia and fabulous mirror here.

PLAY WITH HEIGHT

A potted plant may look all right on the floor, but if you place it on a stool or a pile of books or magazines, it acquires more height and instantly becomes more impressive and jungly. Create a room divider by placing your plants in a plant stand or legged plant boxes. Especially tall, vertically growing plants, like *Sansevieria*, have nice room-dividing characteristics.

opposite: Play with height by using hanging planters as well as tall plant pots.

below, left: How about a *Monstera deliciosa* on your wardrobe? It looks absolutely great in this Berlin home. Additional benefit: It keeps the plant safe from your pets.

below, right: Bibliophiles, listen up! Pile up some of your old books to create extra space for plant displays. Here, a wooden plank adds even more height for this plant collection.

HANGING PLANTS

Instead of placing your plant on a table or the windowsill, hang it from the ceiling. This creates a nice dynamic in a room without taking up precious floor space. The visual effect is extra spectacular if you hang three or more medium or large plants. If your ceiling can't tolerate the weight, you can hang your plants from a curtain rod in front of a window, or run a metal wire between two walls.

left: In a small apartment, stools, side tables, plant stands, and plant hangers are the perfect solutions for freeing up floor space.

opposite: If you are on the handy side, create a floating plant board above your dining table. A simple wooden board, ropes, and trailing plants are all that is needed. For a more sophisticated version, add light fixtures as seen here.

GROUP PLANTS BY TYPE

If you love cactus plants, create a little cactus area with all your potted cacti instead of scattering them around your home at random. Maybe you're a fan of tropical aroid plants and have quite a collection. Place them on a round coffee table in their favorite spot and add your misting device. Pairing plants with similar care needs makes taking care of them so much easier, too.

ADD COLOR

Not a fan of green? Have a look next time you are in a plant shop: There are quite a few plants that come in a variety of colors such as burgundy, pink, red, white, or orange. Create a colorful scene at home with all your non-green plants. Plants with outstanding colors include *Croton*, *Oxalis triangularis*, *Begonia rex*, *Caladium*, *Fittonia*, *Philodendron* 'Pink Princess,' *Tradescantia zebrina* or *T. pallida*, *Hypoestes phyllostachya*, *Echeveria* 'Purple Pearl,' *Coleus*, *Gynura aurantiaca*, and *Aglaonema* 'Pink Anyamanee.'

left: Three *Ficus elastica,* one of them variegated, group together nicely in this Dallas home.

opposite: Plants don't only come in green! This courtyard garden shows off deep shades of purple, pink, and almost black for a stunning color effect.

MAKE A PLANT SHELFIE

What's more fun than a nice shelf filled with personal trinkets and a variety of plants? Unicorns and rainbows? No, seriously, we love a good plant shelfie! Plants can grow up or down, or you can use a plant as a paperweight on a pile of good books, add a nice candle, a travel souvenir, a small clock . . . the options are endless. Plant shelfies are both decorative and practical, as you get to show off utilitarian objects as well as some artistic items.

left: A simple wooden shelf unit looks amazing with a collection of plants in terra-cotta pots. Using the same pot material creates visual unity and makes a stylish statement.

opposite: Plants combine with art, baskets, tribal ceramics, glass domes, and a green backdrop to create the perfect plant shelfie in a home office.

BUILD A BOTANICAL THRONE

When your plants are taken care of, it's time to enjoy their presence and relax: Find a corner in your home and surround your favorite lounge chair with some oversize plants, and keep adding plants until it feels jungly. Then add a coffee table, your favorite drink, and a good book, and sit back and chill. You deserve it!

left: Olive sits on her Insta-famous botanical throne in the company of dog Mylee.

opposite: A reading nook gets the royal treatment with a cozy green velvet armchair framed by a lush fiddle fig, spider plants, aloe vera, and a tall *Kalanchoe beharensis.*

plant tribe stories . . .
Alina Fassakhova

"I love my plants and they love me back."

Location
New York, New York, USA

Profession
Artist

Zodiac
Aquarius

Lives with
Husband Artem and cats Usha and Sofie

Apartment size
400 square feet / 37 square meters

Favorite plant
Monstera deliciosa variegata

Plant decor idea
Hooks for climbing plants are perfect for small spaces and add life to your walls. Invisible cable hooks work perfectly!

Number of plants
More than 50

Instagram
@alina.fassakhova

The dawn of a new day is serene and filled with positive energy in this small and charming apartment on the Upper West Side of Manhattan. High ceilings and beautiful details like carved wooden door frames vie for the eye's attention. But here the competition is tough—more than fifty lush plants create a real urban jungle vibe in this New York City home.

Alina Fassakhova, an artist with Russian roots, lives in this apartment with her husband, Artem, and two jolly cats named Usha and Sofie. Alina's day starts with a morning ritual, and her beloved plants play a crucial role in it.

Whether the day begins with a moody vibe or a cheerful one, Alina's morning ritual ensures she has plenty of positive energy from the earliest hours. Welcoming the day begins with thirty minutes among the plants. Alina checks each plant, watering and pruning the ones that need attention, and gently touching them. It is a mutual experience: She takes care of her plants and her plants take care of her. There is a flow of energy between them that is almost palpable at times. Alina says, "Plants are crucial for me. I start the day with my plants to find inner balance. They help me concentrate and focus. This is a positive energy that comes back to me and fuels my body."

Alina has a deep connection with her plants. As an artist, she draws profound inspiration from them. "I paint surrounded by plants; I cannot imagine any other way. All the shapes, the colors, the lines—everything comes from the natural inspiration that I get from plants. Even though my paintings are now more colorful, the inspiration comes from my plants. Also, after a full day of painting, my eyes need some rest; here, again, the plants come into play. They help me relax and rest my eyes after a long painting session."

Like many plant-filled spaces, Alina's home brims with positive energy and creativity. Her paintings hang above the sofa and lean on the walls; the easel sits in a corner of the living room. Usha and Sofie play; sometimes they roam around or nestle among the plants. A faux fireplace is the absolute eye-catcher, packed with plants from floor to mantel. A faceted mirror multiplies the green effect and draws attention toward the high ceiling.

For Alina, groupings of plants all around the apartment ensure she spends enough time with her greenery. She feels—as many plant owners do—that plants need time and attention in order to thrive. "The more time I spend with my plants," she says, "the better they look. They respond!"

To keep things growing during the somewhat tricky New York winters, Alina uses humidifiers and grow lights. Since grow lights can look a bit too industrial in a beautifully styled home, Alina installs the bulbs in regular light fixtures. It looks great and is a simple and effective solution.

```
opposite, top: Makes your heart skip a
beat: the big heart-shaped leaves of an
Anthurium clarinervium in Alina's home.

opposite, bottom right: A calm moment in
the bedroom with plants and cat Usha.

opposite, bottom left: A quirky figure
plant pot handmade by Spanish ceramicist
Flora Veiga enjoys its spot on Alina's
mantel.
```

plant tribe interview . . .
Maurício Arruda

"The process of growing a plant is what I enjoy most."

Location

São Paulo, Brazil

Profession

Interior designer, architect, television host

Zodiac

Taurus

Instagram

@mauricioarruda

We sat down with Brazilian interior designer Maurício Arruda and asked him three questions about plants in interiors.

What is your personal connection to plants?

For me, plants represent the flow of life and the true sense of being alive to nature and the seasons. Plants keep me balanced in the pace of a huge city like São Paulo. Like caring for pets, cooking, or going to the gym, taking care of my plants reconnects me with the present.

Like many in the Plant Tribe, I see plants less as objects and more as living beings. The process of growing a plant is what I enjoy even more than their aesthetics. I observe them; they talk to me and tell me when something is wrong, or when they need more light or a sip of water. In my plant-filled home I even maintain a little "plant hospital" near the laundry room—a spot I pass multiple times a day, which helps me remember to check on the plants and try to help them feel better.

How do you work with plants in your clients' spaces?

At work, greenery is essential to any new space design. But instead of creating an urban jungle, I work with plants my clients already own—or I propose a small selection of plants that they can grow over time. By starting small, my clients make plants part of their routine and they learn to take life slowly and appreciate a different pace.

Can you tell us more about the Brazilian DNA in design?

This approach to design meshes perfectly with everyday Brazilian life. In general I'd say that Brazilians like to create something extraordinary by using ordinary things. At home we value a warm atmosphere and spend a lot of time with our families and friends. The kitchen is the heart of the home and there are always extra seats or floor cushions for last-minute visitors. In my own home I encourage movement and flow by not owning a coffee table. Because there's no coffee table to gather around, everyone circulates through the living room and sits where they like: on one of the sofas, on a pouf, or near the plant shelves.

opposite: Painting the ceiling a bright green echoes the greenery in the home.

below: A botanical still life with lab flasks, ceramic leaf plates, glass vases, palm tree seedpods, a *Sansevieria* cutting, and some branches.

Tim Labenda

"Our plants grew to our hearts!
They are balm for the soul."

Location

Berlin, Germany

Profession

Creative consultant, designer

Zodiac

Scorpio

Lives with

Boyfriend Hannes and dog Putin

Apartment size

1,290 square feet / 120 square meters

Favorite plant

Fan palm

Plant decor idea

Go for large and mature plants. I prefer
one big plant over ten small ones. A big
plant really makes a statement!

Number of plants

56

Instagram

@timlabenda @hnns.vncnt

The moment you enter the home of Tim and Hannes, in Berlin's Kreuzberg district, you know they are creative souls. Refined furnishings are accentuated with handmade design pieces, and everything is framed with lush tropical plants. The light-filled home is a real jungle—with a fifteen-year-old *Monstera deliciosa* enthroned in the living room and a tall bird-of-paradise swaying in the dining room. Everywhere, fan palms, big philodendrons, and climbing pothos catch the visitor's eye, yet it all seems in perfect balance, clearly the work of an experienced designer.

Tim and Hannes have been living in this spacious apartment for nearly five years now. Their passion for plants was ignited first by the design of a favorite shop—they loved the look and wanted to re-create something similar at home. More inspiration came from the famous Chateau Marmont in Los Angeles. For the creative couple, it became clear—they needed to have an urban jungle at home.

Tim explains their plant shopping strategy this way: "We were very strategic in our choice of plants: We made a wish list knowing exactly what we wanted, then we searched for large, mature examples."

Plants also play a key role in their creative work. "We are both very connected to nature and love being outside," Tim says. "Being in nature replenishes our inspiration. The organic shapes and the different haptic experiences influence our creative process, whether we are designing fashion or home decor. And having plants creates an ongoing light, relaxed, holiday atmosphere at home."

Hannes shares the love for plants with equal vigor and passion. "A home should be an oasis . . . and plants create this feeling—they are a balm for the soul."

opposite, top: The mother plant of all monsteras in their apartment sits in a sunny living room corner.

opposite, bottom left: Plants, dried flowers, and cushions designed by Tim in their breakfast nook.

opposite, bottom right: Plants are a constant inspiration for the couple's creative projects. And coffee is the fuel.

above: Peek in the living room with the fabulous Bocci pendant lamp.

plant tribe stories . . .
Viktoria Dahlberg

"Where there are plants there is love."

Location

Brooklyn, New York, USA

Profession

Designer, photo editor

Zodiac

Virgo

Lives with

Solo

Apartment size

800 square feet / 74 square meters

Favorite plant

Palm trees

Plant decor idea

#plantgang forever <3

Number of plants

11

Instagram

@viktoria.dahlberg
@northfifthandsunny

Life is buzzing in this bright and spacious two-bedroom condo in the heart of Brooklyn's Williamsburg neighborhood. It's home to Viktoria Dahlberg, a Swedish native who moved to the Big Apple five years ago. The delivery guy is a regular at her doorstep, and there are samples of new products patiently waiting to be reviewed and approved. This is where Viktoria works on her fresh home decor brand called N5 & SUNNY, which carries embroidered cushion covers, eco-friendly pillow inserts, and more.

"Plants help me calm down in these busy and stressful times," says Viktoria. "My brand keeps me super busy with long days and that's where plants come into play—they work magic, helping me find my balance when I return home to my Williamsburg apartment." Taking care of her small gang of eleven plants—misting the *Strelitzia nicolai*, watering the golden pothos—encourages her to take it slow and stop thinking about emails, delivery guys, and phone calls.

But plants don't only help Viktoria keep a healthy balance in her life; they also inspire her to create a stylish look for her own lifestyle brand and for clients. "Every photo looks better with some plants! But even if I didn't have to create content for work, I would still live in a minimalist apartment with a lot of houseplants. I grew up in a forest in Sweden, and love for nature is part of my Swedish heritage. I feel best when surrounded by greenery." This is evident throughout her home: a minimalistic white canvas with a dash of textures, playful textile designs, and plants.

Plants move around Viktoria's apartment all the time, according to their needs as well as the needs of styling projects. Four months ago, she bought an oversize cactus (*Cereus peruvianus*) in the Flower District in Manhattan, which came with

a shorter cactus in the same pot. One day it fell over and she realized it was not rooted at all. But it is doing fine now and may grow strong new roots when the days get longer and warmer.

chapter 6

ROOM-BY-ROOM PLANT GUIDE

the living room

Living room detail in the home of Tish Carlson in Albuquerque.

The living room is often the biggest room in a home, with the greatest abundance of natural light. These factors make it an ideal spot for houseplants. In other words, this is the place to go really wild with plants!

Keeping in mind the space you have and the light conditions, opt for any kind of plant that speaks to you. The living room is where a large, mature statement plant has the most potential. Consider a full-grown rubber tree, a tall fiddle-leaf fig, or a big palm tree. Sometimes a single large plant will suffice, but if you want more, go for a variety of leafy plants, such as *Calathea*, ferns, pothos, or varieties of philodendrons placed in different corners. A big *Monstera deliciosa* will be more than happy in a spacious living room, too. Plants are also a good way to camouflage or frame devices, such as a TV, that are not so decorative. Surrounded by plants or plant shelves, any TV will definitely look much cooler and wilder!

Which Plants Will Make a Statement in Your Living Room?

A list of green suggestions to make a botanical statement.

MONSTERA DELICIOSA VARIEGATA

The variegated version of the popular *Monstera* plant has become something like the holy grail of the Plant Tribe. This rare variety is hard to find, and even when you find it, it's pretty pricey. But if you're lucky enough to come across one (or to receive a cutting from a plant friend), don't think twice! Go for it, and put this botanical gem in your living room. Place this beauty in a warm spot that gets bright indirect light and keep it moister than you would its non-variegated cousin. The only risk is that your friends will turn green with envy!

FICUS LYRATA

The fiddle-leaf fig tree makes a great statement plant. For a jungle vibe, go with a mature plant that has big leaves. To encourage fullness, prune the top of the fig, which will force branching on the lower stem. To strengthen the stem, simulate a tropical storm by shaking your plant every now and then (in nature, the wind does the trick). Figs need bright indirect light for healthy growth, and you should clean the leaves regularly to keep them healthy and shiny.

ONE FACT TO KEEP IN MIND:
Don't forget that during the cold months of the year, the living room tends to be the most heated area in a home. The air will be drier then, so you must take simple countermeasures to avoid symptoms of drought: Up your misting game and give your leafy plants a daily spritz of filtered water (tap water will clog the pores and leave annoying watermarks on the leaves).

PHILODENDRON 'PINK PRINCESS'

With its pink leaves, this variegated philodendron is a real eye-catcher, although it is a rarity in plant shops. It is also the perfect addition to a colorful, tropical decorating scheme. A climber, it needs a trellis or other support to vine. Make sure it gets bright indirect light, and keep it on the moist side, with good drainage. Enjoy the pink variegation but make sure to keep it balanced—the pink part has no chlorophyll for the plant to photosynthesize. So you don't want too many all-pink leaves (if that occurs, prune the plant back to the last area of balanced variegation).

STRELITZIA

The famous bird-of-paradise is a beautiful and lush tropical plant that loves bright natural light. Even though this plant hardly ever blooms indoors, it's a real highlight because of its large and long leaves, which sway in a light breeze. Indirect light and some direct sunlight, regular watering, and warmth are optimal for the *Strelitzia*. But watch out: This plant grows quickly and gets pretty tall, so make sure you've allowed enough space for it!

TALL CACTUS OR SUCCULENT

If you prefer a model plant that doesn't branch out too much, opt for a tall cactus or succulent, such as a *Euphorbia trigona* (African milk plant). Keep in mind that these plants require lots of light, and they have thorns and spikes—if you have small kids or pets around, you might want to choose a leafy plant instead.

above, left: A branchy
Monstera adansonii dresses
this Albuquerque, New
Mexico, coffee table.

above, right: For an
instant jungle vibe, go for
mature plants that have big
leaves, like this large
Ficus lyrata.

left: Natural materials
like sustainable wood
and wicker are a perfect
match when decorating with
plants.

right: No need to add dozens of plants to get a jungle feeling in your living room: One tall banana plant and two smaller plants give this nook a green feeling. The dried bouquet and vintage palm leaf table add to its charm.

below: Imagine taking a selfie in this mirror: Lush plants, like this *Monstera deliciosa* (right) and *Rhaphidophora decursiva* (left), will frame your outfit of the day!

the bedroom

For a green shelf above the bed, choose ferns, snake plants, ivy, and trailing philodendrons to create a soothing effect.

Sleeping with Plants

Every time we post a picture of a beautiful bedroom filled with plants on Instagram, we get some concerned comments from readers who believe sleeping in a bedroom with plants is not healthy. Here's why we feel differently: Plants respire as humans do, emitting carbon dioxide at night (the reverse of photosynthesis) and converting carbon dioxide to oxygen (by photosynthesis) during the day. Carbon dioxide (CO_2) and carbon monoxide (CO) are often confused. The names sound similar, both compounds are colorless and odorless gases, and at high concentrations both can be deadly. In small amounts, carbon dioxide is relatively harmless, whereas carbon monoxide is extremely dangerous. Maybe this is the basis of the misperception.

The amount of CO_2 that most plants produce at night is far less than the amount people and pets do. You could even say that sleeping with another person, in the same room or in the same bed, is less healthy (oxygen-wise) than sleeping in a bedroom filled with plants.

The benefits of plants in homes in general, and in bedrooms in particular, are countless. They make a room look more alive, and your bedside table brighter. Taking care of your plants can also help you wind down after a busy day. Studies have even shown that by simply touching the leaf of a plant for two minutes, you reduce your stress levels! For a healthy bedroom regime, don't rely on plants alone, however: Good ventilation, fresh bed linens, a comfortable mattress, good pillows, and an extra blanket, if needed, help you sleep better and improve your overall well-being.

A small *Monstera adansonii* in the Parisian bedroom of Rebecca (see page 122).

right: A floating plant shelfie above the bed features a pothos, a *Hoya linearis*, and a spider plant, among others.

below, left: In bedrooms that are too dark for plants, you can use botanical prints—like this banana leaf pillow cover—to add a jungle vibe.

below, right: Four different snake plants peeking out while the *Sansevieria masoniana* (also known as whale fin snake plant) takes center stage.

Which Plants Are Best for the Bedroom?

As you would before choosing a new plant for any room in your home, first take stock of the light and temperature conditions in your bedroom. If your bedroom is cool and on the dark side, don't pick a plant that requires lots of bright light and warm temperatures.

These are some of our favorite plants for the bedroom:

- The *Sansevieria* plant, also known as the snake plant, is a star in the bedroom: It tolerates low (bedroom) light and thrives on (reasonable) neglect. Did you know that snake plants even convert carbon dioxide to oxygen during the night? This has been shown by several studies and makes this plant number one in your bedroom!

- Aloe vera, a plant of many talents in the home, is a great choice for the bedroom. Not only does it have a sculptural look, it removes benzene and formaldehyde from the air, and its gel helps soothe your skin—in case you have no cream or lotion at your bedside. Just sayin'.

- Another all-around plant is the spider plant, or *Chlorophytum comosum*. It removes toxins from the air, is very easy to care for, and is nontoxic to your pets. So all you pet owners out there, get some spider plants for the bedroom ASAP! Plus, when they grow their own little plant babies, hanging from long runners, they look cool and outer-space-y. So funky!

- For instant style, why not let a *Philodendron* vine grow along your bed canopy or on a wall or the ceiling near your bed? A great look, and the heart-shaped leaves add a subtle romantic touch! Perhaps you're thinking of letting this air-purifying vine grow decoratively above your bed. Why not?!

- Areca palms are yet another great option for the bedroom. Why? Again, they purify the air and are nontoxic to your pets. In addition, they create an instant tropical vibe in your bedroom, transporting you to lush jungles while you dream away. Waking up is like greeting a new day in a tropical paradise! You'll sleep like a baby!

the bathroom

A snake plant and pothos pair neatly with the art in this Portland, Oregon, bathroom.

The Secret to a Sunday-Night Pool Party

When you think of the bathroom, you think of water. Along with the kitchen, it's the place where you fill up your watering can and from which you set off around your home to give all your plants sips of water. But the bathroom is also a very convenient place to treat your plants to a nice shower and let them have their own pool party. The bathtub or shower is the ideal location to clean the leaves of your plants, soak the plants' soil, and allow them time to get rid of excess water via the drainage holes in the pots. It's refreshing for the plants, and if you carefully dry the leaves with a cotton cloth afterward, they'll be fresh and ready for a new round of photosynthesis. When plants are dirty or coated with dust, the plants' pores (called stomata), through which they take in carbon dioxide and release oxygen, become blocked, drastically reducing the leaves' photosynthetic capacity. Rinsing the leaves with water mimics a tropical rainstorm, which some tropical plants, like ferns, truly love. It also washes away accumulated salts from fertilizer and discourages pests, such as spider mites, that thrive in dusty plants. After a shower, it's important that you make sure the soil dries and doesn't stay soggy wet, or the result will be root rot, the primary cause of dead plants. That's also why you should never water your plants in a shower or bathtub if their pots lack drainage holes. It's critical that the water not remain in the pots.

If your plants are in terra-cotta pots, you can fill the bathtub or sink with water to three-quarters of the height of your pots. Place the pots in the water and wait an hour, while the pots and soil soak up the water. Let out the water and allow the pots to air-dry on the outside before returning them to their usual spots in your home. This is a particularly efficient way to water succulents and cacti, which are susceptible to overwatering but whose roots need more water than you expect.

While you're at it, why not turn your bathroom into a green sanctuary for your own private pool party, too? The only requirement is that the room has some natural light, because plants don't grow without light (see page 83). Place your plants on shelves on the wall or on the edge of your bathtub, hang them from the ceiling if you don't have a lot of floor space, add a few on the shelf next to your toothbrush, or even place them in your shower caddy (as long as they're not exposed to any gels and soaps, they'll be fine). Light some candles, pour yourself a glass of your favorite drink, play some music, fill the bathtub or turn on the shower among your plants, and enjoy your party!

Humidity-loving plants like *Aglaonema, Begonia,* Boston ferns, bromeliads, golden pothos, *Nepenthes,* orchids, *Philodendron scandens,* spider plants, staghorn ferns, or *Tillandsia* air plants are ideal for this space.

A *Pilea peperomioides,* a *Calathea concinna* 'Freddie,' an *Opuntia microdasys,* and a *Peperomia angulata* soaking up the sunlight in this Alexandria, Virginia, bathroom.

above, left: A maidenhair fern and ivy thrive in a plant box in the humid bathroom environment.

above, right: A *Calathea* enjoying the extra sunlight on a bathroom windowsill.

right: Philodendrons, bromeliads, and a staghorn fern float above the bathtub in São Paulo.

What If Your Bathroom Has No Windows?

If you absolutely must have plants in a dark bathroom without windows, invest in grow lights that can give your plants what they need more than anything else: full-spectrum light. Or go for a botanical touch in your bathroom that doesn't require living plants: Hang a shower curtain decorated with a foliage pattern, add a *Monstera* leaf–shaped bath mat, install some palm tree–shaped wall hooks, or paint your walls a nice deep green. You can also rotate plants in and out of your bathroom to give them turns at a sunny window elsewhere. Just allow the plants to adapt gradually to each new light situation, as they may shed some leaves or suffer sunburn when the change is too abrupt. We don't recommend faux plants, made of plastic or silk, because they don't grow and because the world doesn't need more plastic.

If you want to avoid unsightly water stains on your plants' leaves, dry the leaves with a cotton cloth immediately after watering. If your water has a high concentration of calcium and other minerals, it can leave a calcium buildup or mineral deposits on porous terra-cotta pots. These are harmless to the plants and give the pots a charming rustic vibe, but they look ugly on leaves (and can possibly clog the stomata). It's best to clean your leaves with a mixture of vinegar or lemon juice and water. Combine one part vinegar or lemon juice with four parts water, soak a cotton cloth in the solution, and wipe the leaves. The calcium should come off fairly easily. Repeat, if necessary.

top: Color coding is a creative way to help organize a shared bathroom.

above: A hanging *Gynura aurantiaca*, also known as purple passion or velvet plant.

the kitchen

Herbs are a classic in the kitchen, but the warm microclimate in this room is good for other houseplants as well, like leafy greens and spiky succulents.

The kitchen is the heart of the house. People gather there, so it's social and it can also be a perfect place for plants. When we cook and bake, we create a certain microclimate in our kitchens. Usually, the kitchen is the place where the temperature and the humidity are higher than in other rooms (except the bathroom). If your kitchen has good natural light, too, then you're good to go for a really wide array of plants to add to the decor.

Bright light, high humidity, and warm temperatures are also the perfect conditions for tropical plants—so don't rule out vining plants and exotics, too. The vines can even be suspended to create a green curtain on walls and ceilings.

Ideal Plants for the Kitchen

A windowsill garden of homegrown herbs—thyme, parsley, rosemary, sage, oregano, lemon balm, and mint—is a natural for this space. But what about some other interesting greens, for the kitchen's wilder side?

CALATHEA LANCIFOLIA

This tropical beauty is commonly known as the rattlesnake plant and adds instant style and a jungle atmosphere. The oblong leaves feature beautiful patterns in shades of deep green and purple. The plant is native to the Brazilian rainforest and thrives in warm and humid environments. Place it in medium to bright indirect light, and keep the pots in your kitchen cooking—a rattlesnake plant loves warm temperatures and high humidity.

MONSTERA ADANSONII

This beautifully perforated plant, commonly known as Swiss cheese plant, grows fast and climbs well.

Place it close to your kitchen window, in bright indirect light, and give it support to climb and thrive. It's very easy to care for: Just water it once the top of the soil has dried. Fertilize every other week during the growth period to keep it green and happy.

ALOCASIA × AMAZONICA 'POLLY'

Commonly known as Amazonian elephant's ear, *Alocasia* prefers semi-shade—perfect for darker corners of your kitchen. Water regularly to keep the moisture level balanced, and keep the area around the plant warm. Take note: For this plant, as for most tropical plants, tap water is too mineralized and will cause spots on the leaves, or even brown tips. Use filtered water or rainwater, when possible!

PHILODENDRON SCANDENS

Here's a great choice if you want a climbing plant to line your walls, your curtain rod, or your kitchen shelves. Commonly called the heart-leaf philodendron, this plant has dark, velvety leaves that thrive in warm, humid places. Put the pot on your shelf and let the plant climb its way through your kitchen! This philo, moreover, is a known air purifier.

MARBLE QUEEN POTHOS

Another great option for a climbing kitchen plant, the Marble Queen pothos (*Epipremnum aureum* 'Marble Queen') is an easy-care plant that will grow even in low light and humidity. It will thrive, however, in bright indirect light and high humidity. Keep the soil on the dry side and you'll have a happy plant.

AVOCADO PLANT

Instead of throwing pits and seeds away, why not grow new plants from them? (See page 101.) An avocado (or mango) plant looks great in a kitchen. And if you eat lots of avocados, you might end up with a little avocado forest on your windowsill, and, hey, why not?!

above, left: A pink orchid adds a touch of color to this stylish counter.

above, right: A fern and lemons create a still life in a Parisian kitchen.

right: Why not try your hand at a little DIY and install a plant shelf in your kitchen?

right: The sun-loving cacti in the windowsill, the leafy greens and spiky succulents in the wall-mounted basket, and the *Monstera adansonii* on the countertop make this kitchen come to life.

below, right: Start the day with freshly brewed coffee in a kitchen framed by plants.

below, left: Plants make a kitchen more inviting and may inspire you to spend more time there as a result. They may even inspire you to spend more time cooking!

kids' rooms

The motto of this home in Albuquerque.

Good Things Grow Here

Start them young! We believe that plants should be part of every room, especially our kids' rooms. Growing up surrounded by plants teaches children valuable lessons about nature and the pace of growth. It's also an opportunity to discuss how our plants, vegetables, and fruit are actually grown, and how they nourish kids' little bodies. The presence of plants creates awareness, even for us adults, that a salad takes time to grow and that the green tomatoes don't taste as good as the bright red, orange, or yellow ones.

Giving your kids responsibility for plant care is an excellent way for them to learn to be patient, to stick to a schedule (to water once every few days, for example), to trust their own judgment (this plant needs water now!), and to appreciate the results of their work. Most kids love having their own houseplants, and learning to care for them can become a family bonding experience. And what about digging in the ground, repotting a few plants, and making a mess? A kid's dream! Go for fast-growing plants that can handle some extra water, and make sure all pots have drainage holes, to avoid root rot if eager tykes water the plants a little more than required. If you have an active family, make sure the plants are safely out of the way on a shelf or the windowsill.

When shopping for plants, involve your kids in the process of picking their new roommates: Do they love speckled plants, say, or the color of that cute variegated rubber plant, or do they prefer a prickly cactus?

Aleksi loves decorating the variegated *Ficus elastica* in his room with some of his koala and teddy bears. His mom, Rebecca, helps add the "tree topper."

below, left: Green accessories and the tones of natural wood establish the color scheme in a cool, botanical-themed room.

bottom, left: A plant shelf holds philodendrons and pothos, and *Dracaena* adds to the mix.

below, right: You are never too young to fall in love with plants. This child's bed is surrounded by mature greenery and decorated with botanical motifs.

bottom, right: Sssshhhh, be quiet.

Growing tomatoes, sunflowers, or alfalfa sprouts in a kid's room isn't usually possible, but there's always space for a few houseplants—here are some kid-friendly ideas.

PILEA PEPEROMIOIDES

Pilea, the Chinese money plant, grows rapidly and produces little babies that can easily be cut off and rooted. *Pilea* babies make cute gifts (they are considered tokens of luck) for friends, especially in customized, kid-decorated plant pots. Or let your kids grow an entire jungle of *Pilea*!

FICUS ELASTICA

Rubber plants are easy growers and—the bigger ones, especially—will make any space feel like a jungle. Make sure your child doesn't break off the plant's leaves, because the milky latex inside is an irritant to the eyes and skin. According to Rebecca's son, Aleksi, the rubber plant is also good for decorating with your favorite plush toys (see page 227).

TILLANDSIA

There is something magical about air plants; they grow without being potted in soil and survive with just a regular spritz of water. This allows for creative plant holders—shells, wire grids, vases, air plant hangers, LEGO creations, or toy figurines.

ASPIDISTRA ELATIOR

The cast-iron plant's name implies it's a tough plant, and it truly is. It doesn't mind a bit of neglect, it looks all right in rooms that provide little light, and it can handle irregular watering and temperature fluctuations.

CYPERUS PAPYRUS

Commonly known as papyrus or paper reed, *Cyperus* is fun to grow. Cut off the top few inches of the stem and place the cutting upside down in a glass of water or well-drained potting mix. The leafy stem tip will be in the water or potting mix, and the leafless portion will point upward toward the ceiling. Roots and new shoots will form over the next few weeks, and soon you will have a new plant. When you have enough papyrus grasses, you can even try to make your own papyrus paper, as the ancient Egyptians used to do.

The dino is amazed by two sweetheart plants (*Hoya kerrii*).

hallways

A thriving *Sansevieria trifasciata*.

Hallways tend to be on the dark side. In most apartments, the hallway is in the back or along the side, with either no windows or low light. Keep that in mind when selecting plants. If your hallway has an abundance of bright natural light, feel free to pick plants that you like and that suit your interior style. If it's dark, choose accordingly.

Which Plants Will Thrive in Your Dark Hallway?

Plants that can handle semi-shade are the best option for your dark hallway. Here's a list of our favorites:

SANSEVIERIA

The famous snake plant comes in different variations if you're bored with the classic look. Why not try the *Sansevieria* 'Moonlight' (sometimes called *Sansevieria* 'Moonshine'), with its pale silver leaves? Snake plants can tolerate very low light and will add a green touch to dark hallways. In addition, their upright leaves ensure that, in small and narrow passageways, they won't take up too much space.

RHAPIS EXCELSA

This plant, commonly known as the lady palm, usually grows in tropical forests under a canopy of larger trees; thus, it's used to low light. It's a great option if your hallway gets only low indirect light (but don't place it in a corner with no light at all).

ZAMIOCULCAS ZAMIIFOLIA

The *Zamioculcas zamiifolia*, or ZZ plant, is perfect for low-light corners of your hall. Don't overwater this plant, especially when it's placed in a shaded corner. Make sure you have some space, as it tends to spread as it grows.

SPIDER PLANT

The spider plant, *Chlorophytum comosum*, is a fine option for any low-light area of your home. It's also a great choice if you have limited space, as you can simply put it in a plant hanger.

LUCKY BAMBOO

Another great option for low light, lucky bamboo, *Dracaena sanderiana*, can be grown in water only, so you can arrange a few vases of lucky bamboo on your hallway table. Another reason this plant is great for a hallway is because it's said to attract luck and good fortune. Yes, please come in!

Sansevieria are staple plants for areas in your home that tend to be on the dark side, like hallways. They are happy in brighter light, but can survive in lower light conditions.

room-by-room plant guide

this page: Pothos is a
hallway favorite, as
seen in these Manhattan
(above) and Brooklyn
(right) apartments.

opposite: Hallways tend
to be darker and narrow,
so choose plants that
can handle low light and
do not take up too much
space (such as snake
plants).

End Note: Helping Your Plants Survive Your Vacation

Summertime! Time to leave your urban jungle and go on a well-deserved vacation or visit friends or family. You've packed your sunglasses, beach towel, and a few books? Then it's time to prepare your plants for a few days or weeks without your care. Don't stress—we have some tips so that your houseplants will survive your vacation.

above: A simple idea to keep your plants healthy during your absence: a self-watering wick system.

opposite: Unwind during your vacation— your plants will be safe and happy at home.

FIND A PLANT SITTER. Ideally, ask someone you trust to take care of your plants. Maybe a neighbor or friend can visit once a week, or more often, if needed, and give your plants some water and some fresh air (by opening the windows). Make it easier for your sitter by providing information about how much water your plants need, along with other specific plant care instructions. Be creative: You can use little flags or colored stickers to mark plants that need a lot of water, or extra fertilizer, or misting. Even easier, just make a short video with your smartphone and send it to your plant-sitting friend! Be sure to explain what "a lot of water" or "very little water" means: Is it one cup per week, or an entire watering can per plant?

MAKE CERTAIN YOUR PLANTS ARE HEALTHY. Some plants may need fresh potting soil or soil aeration (see page 119). Check your plants for bugs and diseases, too. Treat accordingly before you leave. Or place the infested plants in quarantine.

GROUP YOUR PLANTS. This makes watering easier for your plant sitter and increases the air humidity slightly, should you decide to go for a self-watering option. And bonus points: A plant gang looks very stylish, too.

SOME PLANTS, LIKE FICUS PLANTS, DON'T LIKE TO BE MOVED, so don't move them just for your vacation. If you really want to group a plant with your other houseplants, move it gradually during the weeks before your departure.

PLANTS NEED LIGHT AND WATER to stay alive, even more so in the summer, when they're growing. So don't place your plants in a dark room with the shutters closed! An airy room with medium light—and no direct sunlight, to avoid sunburn—is better.

REMEMBER THAT MORE PLANTS DIE OF OVERWATERING than under-watering, so placing them in a bathtub filled with water, which is sometimes suggested as a solution to keep your plants alive during a trip, is not always ideal.

USEFUL TOOLS. There are numerous tools on the market that can help your plants survive a few days or weeks without care. For example, at any garden center, you can find automatic drip irrigation systems, often with settings that can be programmed to provide customized watering for your plants while you're away. But there are also some reliable nonelectric, more stylish solutions for your plants. Below you'll find some of our personal favorites:

- TERRA-COTTA WATERING CONES (also called spikes or stakes). These devices, unglazed or partially glazed, can be used in combination with an empty glass bottle, such as a wine bottle, to provide water during your vacation.

- WATERING GLOBES AND CERAMIC OYA (also known as watering bulbs). Globes come in glass, ceramic, or PVC, and you simply fill up the reservoir with water, turn the globe upside down, and stick it into the soil, close to the roots of your plant. Similar to watering cones, watering globes slowly release water into the soil. For large plants, you may want to use two or more watering globes so all the roots get watered evenly.

- SHOELACE METHOD. All you need is a glass, mug, or other vessel and an old shoelace. Fill the glass with water, and place one end of the shoelace in the glass and the other end in the soil of your plant. The shoelace transports the water slowly from the vessel to the pot and ensures constant hydration without overwatering your plant. Perfect and easy! This simple method is suitable for smaller houseplants.

- WATER-STORING CRYSTALS, also known as water-retaining gel or hydrogel. This isn't an organic method, as the crystals contain polymers, so we don't use it very often. The crystals contain up to three weeks' worth of water. You simply position them on the soil, or mix them with the upper layer of the soil if you don't like the look of the gel. They'll absorb and release water throughout your vacation. We advise testing this method before you go away, so that you know the exact amount of gel your plants need.

- SELF-WATERING POTS. These include pots with integrated wicks that transport water from reservoirs to the soil and roots, terra-cotta pots bathing in cachepots filled with water, and planters with water reservoirs integrated into their liners. Self-watering pots make going on vacation a breeze. They are also very convenient throughout the year.

Resources

AUSTRALIA

Foliage Plant Studio
237 Grange Rd.
Findon, SA 5023
@foliage_plantstudio

Ivy Muse
1250 High St.
Armadale, VIC 3143
@ivymuse_melb

Little Leaf Co
4 / 496 Marmion St.
Myaree, WA 6154
@littleleafco

Plant by Packwood
60 Rose St.
Fitzroy, VIC, 3065
@plantbypackwood

Unveiling Poppy
Shop 8a, 3 Cupania St.
Daisy Hill, QLD 4127
@unveilingpoppystore

ZZ Botanical and Home
172 Ferguson St.
Williamstown, VIC 3016
@zzbotanicalandhome

BELGIUM

Agave
Rue de Dublin 15
1050 Ixelles
@agave_boutique

Brut
Rue Haute 202
1000 Bruxelles
@brutbrussels

Gruun
Oud Korenhuis 36
Pl. de la Vieille Halle
aux Blés 36
1000 Bruxelles
@gruunbxl

Jangala Shop
En Neuvice 28
4000 Liège
@jangalashop

Little Green Stories
Sint-Jacobsnieuwstraat
82 9000 Gent
@littlegreenstories

Stek
Nederkouter 129
9000 Gent
@stekgent

The Plant Corner
Isabellalei 144
2018 Antwerpen
@theplantcorner

BRAZIL

Bloom Espaço Botânico
Rua Cassimiro de Abreu,
56, Brisamar João
Pessoa
@bloomjp

Blumenfee Floricultura
Rua Treze de Maio,
485, Bela Vista
São Paulo
@blumenfee_floricultura

Botânica e Tal
Rua Major Sertório,
92, República
São Paulo
@botanicaetal

FLO Atelier Botânico
Rua Delfina, 115
São Paulo
@floatelierbotanico

Jardin do Centro
Rua General Jardim
490-494, São Paulo
@jardindocentro

Petit Jardin
St. de Habitações
Coletivas e Geminadas
Norte, 715, Bloco B
Casa 30
Brasília
@ton.petit.jardin

Plantestilo
CLS, 402, Bloco A, Loja
15 Brasília
@plantestilo

Selvvva
Ave. Angélica, 501,
Térreo
São Paulo
@selvvva

Terra Jardim Ateliê Botânico
Alameda Jaú,
1906, Jardim Paulista
São Paulo
@terrajardim

Verdeiro Josephina
Rua Horácio Lane, 205
São Paulo
@verdeirojosephina

CANADA

Crown Flora Studio
1233 Queen St. W
Toronto, ON M6 K1L5
@crownflora

Dynasty
1086 1/2 Queen St.
Toronto, ON M6J 1H8
@dynastytoronto

Stamen & Pistil Botanicals
1567 Dundas St W
Toronto, ON M6K 1T9
@stamenandpistilbotan-
icals

CHILE

El Bazar del Jardínista
Ave. Providencia 1336,
Local 47
Santiago 7500000
@el_jardinista

The Plant Store
Nueva Providencia 2212
Santiago 7510086
@theplantstorestgo

CZECH REPUBLIC

Pokoj
Schnirchova 1257 / 4
Prague, 170 00
@pokoj.store

DENMARK

Butanik
Classensgade 10
2100 København
@butanikcph

Kaktus København
Jægersborggade 35
2200 København
@kaktus_kbh

Plant København
Århusgade 132, 2150
Nordhavn Jægersborggade
27, 2200 København N
@plant_kbh

Planteplaneter
Stefansgade 12
2200 København N
@planteplaneter

Stalks and Roots
Vendersgade 5
1363 København
@stalksandroots

FRANCE

Green Factory
17 Rue Lucien Sampaix,
75010 Paris/
98 Rue des Dames,
75017 Paris
@green_factory

Ikebanart
49 Rue Lucien Sampaix
75010 Paris
@ikebanart

Jane Jardinerie
10 Rue Mercœur,
44000 Nantes/
21 Rue Toussaint,
49100 Angers
@jane_jardinerie

Le Cactus Club
29 Rue de la Fontaine
au Roi 75011 Paris
@lecactusclub

Leaf
46 Rue Albert Thomas
75010 Paris
@leaf.paris

Les Succulents Cactus
111 Rue de Turenne
75003 Paris
@lessucculentscactus

Mama Petula
74 Ave. Denfert-Rochereau
75014 Paris
@mamapetula

What The Flower
35 Rue du Chemin Vert
75011 Paris
@whattheflower_paris

GERMANY

Hallesches Haus
Tempelhofer Ufer 1
10961 Berlin
@hallescheshaus

Plant Circle
Allerstraße 11
12049 Berlin
@plantcircle

The Botanical Room
Manteuffelstraße 73
10999 Berlin
@thebotanicalroom

The Greens
Am Krögel 2 10179
Berlin
@thegreensberlin

Winkel van Sinkel
Wexstraße 28, 20355
Hamburg
Grindelberg 62,
20155 Hamburg
@winkelvansinkel_hh

GREECE

Kopria Store
Eresou 30 Athens 10681
@kopriastore

ISRAEL

GRDN Plant Shop
29 Nahalat Binyamin 29
Tel Aviv
@grdn_tlv

Makers
Maze St. 4
Tel Aviv
@tlvmakers

ITALY

Wild
Via Giuseppe Sirtori,
11 20129 Milano
@wildmilano

THE NETHERLANDS

De Balkonie
Jan Evertsenstraat 90H
1056 EG Amsterdam/
Javastraat 115
1094 HD Amsterdam
@debalkonie

Filya Indoor Garden
Fluwelen Burgwal 1F
2511 CH Den Haag
@filyaindoorgarden

Greennest Gallery
Budapestlaan 17
3584 CV Utrecht
@howareyougrowing

Groene Vingers
Burgwal 23 2611 GE
Delft
@groenevingersdelft

Oerwoud
Vughterstraat 84
5211GL Den Bosch
@oerwouddenbosch.nl

Plantaardig
Zusterstraat 10
4331 KJ Middelburg
@plantaardigmiddelburg

Rood&Bloem
Springweg 14
3511 VP Utrecht
@roodenbloem

Stek de Stadstuinwinkel
Nieuwe Binnenweg 195b
3021 GA Rotterdam
@stekdestadstuinwinkel

Wildernis
Bilderdijkstraat 165F
1053 KP Amsterdam
@wildernisamsterdam

Wonderwoud
Boschstraat 75a
6211 AV Maastricht
@wonderwoud

NORWAY

Planterommet
Strandgaten 80 5004
Bergen
@planterommet

RUSSIA

Änta's
Borovaya 116
Saint Petersburg
@a.n.t.a.s

Krapiva Krapiva
Prospekt Mira 12 c 2
Moscow
@krapivakrapiva

Plant Me
Ulica Zacepa 21,
str3 Moscow
@plantmemoscow

SOUTH AFRICA

Angles+Earth
5 Harman Rd.
Claremont, Cape Town
@ae_terrariums

Opus
Shop 3A, Silo 3, Fish
Quay Rd.
V&A Waterfront
Cape Town
@opusbotanicalstudio

SPAIN

Cacto Cacto
Calle Fernando VI, 7
28004 Madrid
@cacto.cacto

Casa Protea
Carrer de Ramón y
Cajal, 124
08024 Barcelona
@casaprotea

Espai Joliu
Carrer de Badajoz 95
08005 Barcelona
@espaijoliu

Planthae
Calle del Dr. Fourquet,
30
28012 Madrid
@planthae

TURKEY

La Planta
Kuzguncuk Mah. İcadiye
Cad. Behlül Sk. No: 7A
34674 Üsküdar Istanbul
@laplantadesign

Plantsta Botanik & Cafe
Mustafa Kemal Paşa
Mahallesi
Atatürk Cd. No: 71/A
35310
Güzelbahçe İzmir
@plantstacom

UK

Botany
5 Chatsworth Rd.
London E5 0LH
@botanyshope5

Root Houseplants
The Bluecoat, School
Ln.
Liverpool L1 3BX
@root_houseplants

The Plant Point
Corn Exchange Balcony,
Call Ln.
Leeds LS1 7BR /
38 Leeds Road
Ilkey LS29 8DS
@theplantpoint

Conservatory Archives
493-495 Hackney Rd.,
London E2 9ED /
3-7 Lower Clapton Rd.,
London E5 0NS
@conservatory_archives

Flourish Manchester
8A Tib St.
Manchester M4 1PQ
@flourish_manchester

Prick
492 Kingsland Rd.
Dalston London E8 4AE
@prickldn

Forest
43 Lordship Ln.
London SE22 8EW /
Arch 133, Deptford
Market Yard
London SE8 4NS
@forest_london

Dahlia
17 Roseneath St.
Edinburgh EH9 1JH
@dahliathestore

USA

Arium Botanicals
2808 NE Martin Luther
King Jr. Blvd., Suite 3
Portland, OR 97212
@ariumbotanicals

Dahing Plants
289 Grand St.
New York, NY 10002

Fern Shop Cincinnati
6040 Hamilton Ave.
Cincinnati, OH 45224
@fernshopcincinnati

Flora/Fauna
751 Gaskill St. SE
Atlanta, GA 30316
@florafaunaatl

Folia Collective
5117 Eagle Rock Blvd.
Los Angeles, CA 90041
@foliacollective

Green Fingers Market
5 Rivington St.
New York, NY 10002
@greenfingersmarket

Greenery NYC
91 West St.
Brooklyn, NY 11222
@greenerynyc

Gurton's Plant Shop
6360 SW Capitol Hwy.
Portland, OR 97239
@gurtonsplantshop

Homecoming
107 Franklin St.
Brooklyn, NY /
92 Berry St.
Brooklyn, NY
@homecoming

Hot Cactus
1505.5 Echo Park Ave.
Los Angeles, CA 90026
@hotcactus_la

Little Lula Rose
3225 E Colfax Ave.
Denver, CO 80206
@littleluladenver

No Longer Wander Shop
10301 Comanche Rd. NE,
Suite 3
Albuquerque, NM 87111
@nolongerwandershop

Oasis Plant Shop
416 W 8th St.
Dallas, TX 75208
@oasisplantshop

Opuntia Cafe
922 Shoofly St.
Santa Fe, NM 87505
@opuntiacafe

Other Times Vintage
48 Bogart St.
Brooklyn, NY 11206
@othertimesvintage

Paiko Hawaii
675 Auahi St.
Honolulu, HI 96813
@paikohawaii

Pistils Nursery
3811 N Mississippi Ave.
Portland, OR 97227
@pistilsnursery

Plant Shed
1 Prince St.
New York, NY 10012
@plantshednyc

Redenta's Garden Shop
2001 Skillman St.
Dallas, TX 75206
@redentas

Rooted
81 Quay St.
Brooklyn, NY 11222
@rootednyc

Ruibal's Plants of Texas
601 S Pearl Expy.
Dallas, TX 75201
@ruibalsgardenshop

Scape Supply
2211 N Beckley Ave.
Dallas, TX 75208
@scapesupply

Solabee Flowers & Botanicals
801 N Killingsworth St.
Portland, OR 97217
@solabeeflowers

Sprout Home Brooklyn
59 Grand St.
Brooklyn, NY 11249
@sprouthomebrooklyn

Sprout Home Chicago
745 N. Damen Ave.
Chicago, IL 60622
@sprouthomechicago

Starflower
3564 SE Hawthorne Blvd.
Portland, OR 97214
@starflowerpdx

Stonefruit Espresso
1058 Bedford Ave.
Brooklyn, NY 11205
@stonefruitespresso

Stump Plants
305 E 5th Ave.
Columbus, OH /
220 Thurman Ave.
Columbus, OH /
956 N 2nd St.
Philadelphia, PA /
Van Aken District
Cleveland, OH
@stumpplants

Tend Greenpoint
252 Franklin St.
Brooklyn, NY 11222
@tendgreenpoint

The Sill
84 Hester St.
New York, NY /
448 Amsterdam Ave.
New York, NY /
8125 W 3rd St.
Los Angeles, CA /
2181 Union St.
San Francisco, CA
@thesill

The Victorian Atlanta
675 Ponce De Leon
Ave.
Atlanta,GA 30308
@thevictorianatlanta

The ZEN Succulent
121 Market St.
Suite 203
Durham, NC 27701 /
208 S Wilmington St.
Raleigh, NC 27601
@thezensucculent

Utsuwa Floral Design
1288 Polk St.
San Francisco, CA 94109
@utsuwafloraldesign

Wild Island Collective
3504 Adams Ave.
San Diego, CA 92116
@wildisland.collective

Tylor and Anthony,
Arium Botanicals,
Portland, Oregon

plant tribe authors . . .

Igor Josifovic

Location

Munich, Germany

Zodiac

Taurus

Favorite plant

Ficus lyrata

Instagram

@igorjosif

Bio

Igor Josifovic is a social media consultant focusing on interior design, home decor, travel, and plants. With Judith de Graaff, he is the co-author of the bestselling book *Urban Jungle* (Callwey Verlag, 2016) and co-founder of the Urban Jungle Bloggers community.

@urbanjungleblog
urbanjunglebloggers.com

Judith de Graaff

Location

Nogent-sur-Oise, France

Zodiac

Leo

Favorite plant

Totem pole cactus

Instagram

@joelixjoelix

Bio

Judith de Graaff is a freelance designer living near Paris, with a focus on interior design, travel, color, and plants. With Igor Josifovic, she is the co-author of the bestselling book *Urban Jungle* (Callwey Verlag, 2016) and co-founder of the Urban Jungle Bloggers community.

@urbanjungleblog
urbanjunglebloggers.com

plant tribe photographer . . .

Jules Villbrandt

Location

Berlin, Germany

Zodiac

Libra

Favorite plant

Begonia maculata

Instagram

@herz.und.blut

Bio

Jules Villbrandt is a creative mind and photographer from Berlin, always on the hunt for something new in design and art for her blog, herzundblut.com.

Acknowledgments

Thank you, Jules—it has been a dream to work and travel together, and we absolutely adore the beautiful photography that you created for this book.

Thank you to Judy, Shawna, Heesang, and the entire Abrams team for believing in us, and for bearing with us and our relentlessness from time to time. This book would not be what it is without you.

Thank you to these wonderful people: Viktoria, Alina, Artem, Theodora, Benjamin, Tim, Hannes, Juliette, Gaëtan, Louison, Rebecca, Aleksi, Ben, Jennifer, Julie, Brooks, Asa, William, Andy, Tylor, Anthony, Tish, Matt, Kelsey, Audrey, Grayson, Olive, Rudy, Lucas, Renato, Toy, Derek, Michell, Felipe, Júlia, Renata, Maurício, Octávio, Samantha, Fanny, and all their furry companions.

I am thankful for all the ongoing love and support I receive from so many people. This love is my engine, my source of inspiration and strength, my reason to laugh, to work, and to go that extra mile. I also want to apologize to all of them for my lack of time and attention, for my frayed nerves at times and frequent absence during the book-writing process. Merci to my plant partner Judith for bearing with me, my chaos and confusion, and all the late-night chats and calls, as well as to Robert for trusting me with his wife during a three-week-long production trip. With this book I hope I can return some of the love to all of them and beyond—to the entire Plant Tribe out there! You all made this happen. I am humbled and grateful. Dedicated to Cleber.

—Igor

Merciii to Robert for his unconditional love, patience, and Fifth Beatle support; to my dear family for their enthusiasm and confidence in me; to Simone for his precious advice and humor; to my Mastermind buddies (Anne, Cécile, Catherine, Clotilde, Jane) for their guidance. Merci to Igor, the best partner in green crime that I could wish for. Thank you for making Urban Jungle Bloggers such a fun, crazy, and green adventure, and for teaching me over and over again that sleep is overrated. And thank you to the entire Plant Tribe for sharing your love and stories. It is so heartwarming!

—Judith